# GUERRILLA WARFARE FOR TEACHERS
(A Survival Guide)

by

Evan Keliher, Ed.D.

Pedagogue Press P.O. Box 28808 San Diego, California 92198

All rights reserved. No part of this work may be reproduced or transmitted in any form or by any means, electronic or mechanical, including photocopying, recording, or by any information storage and retrieval system without written permission from the author, except for the inclusion of brief attributed quotations in a review.

Evan Keliher ©1995
(Rev. Ed.) 2010
Cover & Layout by – Big Mean Lady
bigmeanlady.webs.com
ISBN: 978-0-9648859-5-0
Library of Congress Catalog
Card Number: 95–71836

To All Readers: The author and Pedagogue Press shall have neither liability nor responsibility to any person or entity with respect to any loss or damage caused, or alleged to be caused, directly or indirectly, by the information contained in this work. Author and Pedagogue Press are particularly opposed to any illegal or violent acts and in no way encourage readers to do anything that is illegal in law or in any way violates the rights of any person.

Printed in the United States of America

## Other works by Evan Keliher

### BOOKS

BOOMERS!
(A Survival Guide for the Future)

Grandpa's Marijuana Handbook

The De-Balling of America

Tyrannicide
(The Story of the Second American Revolution)

Lust Busters

Grandpa Ganja's
High School Survival Guide

### FILMS / VIDEOS

Rebel High (*feature film*) Montreal, Canada

My Lovely Bank (*sitcom pilot*) Montreal, Canada

Grandpa's Marijuana Handbook (*the movie*)
San Diego, CA

### PLAYS

Sandwiched Light

Witte's End

Additional sitcoms/plays/screenplays
www.grandpaspotbook.com

# GUERRILLA WARFARE FOR TEACHERS

## TABLE OF CONTENTS

| Chapter | Page |
|---|---|
| America's Teachers Are | 6 |
| Introduction | 8 |
| 1  Surviving Study Hall | 11 |
| 2  Gird Your Loins for the Perils of Extra-Curricular Duty | 17 |
| 3  Tricks for Out-Dueling Ninth-Graders | 31 |
| 4  How to Foil Hooky Players | 43 |
| 5  Summer School and Dante's Inferno | 53 |
| 6  You and God | 57 |
| 7  Savor Little Victories for Your Health's Sake | 61 |
| 8  Thwarting Snoopervisors | 65 |
| 9  Surviving the Dreaded Teachers' Meeting | 69 |
| 10  Parents' Night | 74 |
| 11  How to Use Sick Days | 78 |
| 12  A Failed Strategy For Recapturing the School Johns | 81 |
| 13  The Counselor: Friend or Foe? | 95 |
| 14  Catching Cheaters | 103 |
| 15  Guns and How to Live with Them | 112 |

| 16 | The Pitfalls of Substitute Teaching | 120 |
|---|---|---|
| 17 | Teaching Outside Your Major | 126 |
| 18 | Beware the Dangers of Sex Education | 130 |
| 19 | Pay and Perks | 139 |
| 20 | Vouchers | 146 |
| 21 | The Chaining of the Doors | 150 |
| 22 | Getting Promoted | 157 |
| 23 | Assorted Discipline Dodges | 162 |
| 24 | School Reform: A Waste of Time | 180 |
| 25 | Professional Organizations | 187 |
| 26 | The Office Staff | 190 |
| 27 | Principals | 194 |
| 28 | How to Downsize Your Superintendent – And Why | 202 |
| 29 | How One Victim Got Even | 208 |
| 30 | Teacher Types – An Overview | 209 |
| | A Survival Kit | 215 |
| | A Final Word | 217 |

## AMERICA'S TEACHERS ARE...

...underpaid, unloved, and unsung. To add injury to insult, the job is downright dangerous, the stress high and morale low. Teachers are routinely threatened, vilified, thrown down the stairs and out of windows, insulted by their administrators, and blamed for the nation's growing ignorance.

Yet they persist. Most of our kids do learn something in the public schools, even the so-called worst ones, and that happens because a lot of people are good at their jobs and manage to succeed in spite of all the obstacles put in their way by irresponsible kids, misguided parents, half-witted administrators, cynical politicians, and an apparent national disinclination to apply common sense where needed.

Guerrilla Warfare for Teachers is the only book ever written that reveals the truth about American education and offers specific changes to address its myriad problems. Issues of merit pay, administrative failures, low achievement, curricular matters, failed methodologies, vouchers, charter schools, the myth of so-called bad teachers and schools, dropout and low graduation rates and more are examined with an eye to revealing the truth rather than the current alibis and outright lies by those anxious to advance their own interests.

There is, in fact, nothing at all wrong with our public schools; they are precisely what they have always been and are not subject to much in the way of change.

NB—please note that this work is based on my thirty-year career in some of the worst schools on the planet. The building was on fire several times a week, sporadic gunfire punctuated the fire drills, daily attendance ran about 70%, many teachers became stoners by inhaling the pot smoke seeping from the johns, half of the kids never graduated, and it's still exactly the same thirty years after I left the place. Forewarned is forearmed.

Even so, the advice contained herein is the best you'll ever receive and well worth its weight in, well, whatever good ideas are worth.

## INTRODUCTION

I was a teacher for thirty years and liked both teaching and teachers. The teachers I knew were hard working, capable pros who really cared and did their level best to help the kids learn.

They worked in a hostile environment, one that was often dangerous, their cars were stolen at regular intervals, powerful chemicals drifted through the air vents and fried their brains like a pan of eggs, and they earned shameful wages and little respect. But they were, and still are, pros.

I was a witness when the system began to fall apart. The kids took charge of the schools in the 'sixties aided and abetted by lunatic-fringe types posing as concerned parents or community activists. School boards surrendered power to anyone who demanded some, superintendents sold out in droves, school administrators wrung their hands and all of them blamed the teachers for the resulting chaos.

Teachers barely surviving as it is thus get an undeserved bad rap and nobody goes to bat for them. I thought it was time someone did and this book is the result.

My story begins with my transfer to Mackenzie High School after stints in elementary and junior high schools. Mackenzie is a large high school deep in the inner city of Detroit, an old building in good repair and actually functioning fairly well overall. The school had churned out reasonably well-educated grads for forty years and was still doing so when I arrived in '65.

Alas, all that changed soon enough. Maybe it was the war or marijuana or crazy rock bands or whatever but almost overnight Mackenzie High turned into an educational nightmare. We had riots and fires and marijuana smoke-ins on a regular basis. Cops were assigned to patrol our halls along with a dozen security guards and all available teachers. Entering students passed through metal detectors, vandals vandalized everything in sight, and muggers mugged.

Test scores fell along with morale. Nobody knew what the hell was going on or what he should do about it. A new principal was sent in to fix things and he didn't last a whole semester before riots and chaos sent him packing. A procession of replacements followed him. Teachers were assaulted and abused; many were driven into early retirement or homes for the unstable. It was the beginning of what many regard as the end of public education in America, a long slide into mediocrity and intellectual malaise.

This, then, is the author's eyewitness account of this continuing decline and the lessons learned from it. The teachers at Mackenzie High not only survived, they even flourished in this academic maelstrom and they did it in classic fashion by employing the hit-and-run guerrilla tactics used by underdogs everywhere. You can survive, too, if you memorize and apply the Survival Rules herein.

These Survival Rules are spread throughout the text to provide readers with concrete ideas for getting through the experience alive and in more or less one piece. These Rules were garnered from thirty years of teaching in some of the worst schools on the planet and all have been field-tested. If you can reject idealism for realism, the way things ought to be for the way they are, madness for sanity, then this book can easily give you the edge you need to survive in the frontlines of modern American education and beat the rascals at their own game.

Certain chapters relating to my experiences at Mackenzie have been interspersed to provide actual eyewitness accounts of the madness and mayhem our staff was required to live with and still is to this day. Some of these incidents have been exaggerated for dramatic effect but not by much.

While humor and satire are employed to entertain the reader even as he's informed, GWFT is the most serious of books, as it attempts to make our schools better for kids, teachers, and society.

We'll take things in no particular order and without apparent rhyme or reason just as they occur in real life. We begin with an overview of study halls at the Big Mack and finish when we get to the end.

*The things taught in school are not an education,
but a means to an education.*
— Ralph Waldo Emerson

## Chapter One

### SURVIVING STUDY HALL

Most schools employ the use of study halls as a logistical way to accommodate those students who have a blank slot in their schedules and need someplace to go between classes. In former times a study hall was just that, a place to study. Kids would bring their books and at least one #2 pencil and actually use the time to do their homework or read or doodle or whatever.

The point is it was a simple job for the teacher, one that required little effort and even offered a chance to catch a few winks if done subtly. The kids would grind away in utter silence, a large clock would tick off the passing minutes with a sound audible out into the hall, and life was ever so pleasant.

Well, not anymore. Study halls at Mackenzie bear little resemblance to such serene settings. These rooms are double-sized classrooms outfitted with five rows each containing some twenty desks bolted to the floor. There is a teacher's desk at the front of the room and most study halls have a glass-enclosed counselor's cubicle at one end. The counselor always faces away from the study hall and keeps the door tightly closed to keep out the noise and any flying debris.

As you can see, if each desk held one person you'd have somewhere in the neighborhood of 100 kids in a given study hall and when we're talking about today's so-called students we're talking real trouble.

Nobody studied in our study halls; such a thing was not possible. For one thing, nobody brought books or pencils, paper, notes or homework. Each student brought himself and an attitude, nothing more. The rule was there were no rules.

People talked right out loud. They shouted to each other. Peals of laughter rent the air. Airborne objects crisscrossed the room as kids threw each other sundry items of apparel, war, and food. They walked around the room at will, sat in the wrong seats, played cards, disappeared altogether for long stretches, and generally did whatever they damn well pleased.

And how does the teacher deal with this madness? Shrewdly, if she's shrewd. Remember, our interest is in mere survival. We only care about staying out of the emergency ward and getting that pension. No heroics for us.

It's a good idea not to confront anybody. Kids today don't like to hear the word no; it irritates them and encourages resentment and even hostility. Still, you want to make a show of getting order so they won't think you're a wuss and run you out of the building and clear out of the profession. This requires certain acting talents and just the right amount of verve.

*Survival Rule:* **To avoid study halls, forge a note from your doctor claiming you're allergic to noise.**

First, close off that rear door if you have one with some of that tape cops use to secure crime scenes. There's always lots of this tape around the campus so you won't have to bring any of your own. This means the kids have to leave by the door nearest your desk and you'll have a better chance to keep track of who comes and goes in case the police later need your testimony as to a given kid's whereabouts.

Okay, the first kids arrive and you have to set the stage. And don't forget we're guerrillas now. Take them by surprise. Hit them when they least expect it.

Stand at the door and glare at them as they enter. Show them you mean business and won't take any crap and maybe you can intimidate some of the weaker ones.

Once they're all inside and before the first riot gets underway, write the words "Shut Up!!!" in big block letters on the chalkboard for all to see. Nobody will shut up, of course, but it shows you're a pro and nobody's fool.

Incidentally, you have to make a speech about here but first you have to do something about the noise or your hearing will fail and leave you deaf as a post. An hour a day in such a din is comparable to an eight-hour shift in a foundry where twelve-ton presses crash down on steel drums every eight seconds. Such noise can almost be seen with the naked eye or actually felt with a bare hand.

One idea widely used at the Big Mack was to stuff cotton balls in your ears and wear headphones over the cotton, a combination that reduced the noise level by a hundred or more decibels. One teacher, Jan Cramer from English, used the headphones to drown out the noise with loud rock music but that didn't work too well as the music itself produces deafness. Still, it was better to go deaf listening to music than to the awful sounds produced in the average study hall.

In any case, when you can make yourself heard, make this speech and put them on notice that you're not going to take that crap mentioned above.

"This is a study hall. If you don't have your books, put your head down and go to sleep. No talking. No eating. No hall passes. No radios. No smoking. No cards. No twittering. No semaphore flags. Raise your hand if you have a question. Are there any questions?"

If any hands are raised, ignore them.

Scowl fiercely. Keep one hand in your coat pocket to hint you may have a gun. Marv Nussbaum, a teacher in my department, kept a large stapler in his pocket and let it bang against a desk or a passing kid from time to time and everybody thought he had a 9mm pistol in there. Sometimes he used big toy bullets as worry beads to heighten the phony gun impression.

Carry a pointer, one without the usual rubber tip, and make slashing moves with it à la Zorro carving his initials on miscellaneous chests. As you move about the room stop and whirl around suddenly every now and again to catch the kids who give you the finger or stick out their tongues after you've passed them. If you catch one in the act send him to his counselor for discipline and make a great show of it so the others will be more tractable in order to avoid visiting their own counselors.

No, the counselor won't really do anything to the kid but you don't care about that. What you want is that particular kid the hell out of your way at this particular moment and you don't care where he goes or what he does as long as he's somewhere else. Things like justice and fair play are abstractions and no concern of yours. Survival is all you care about.

Another device that works is to order each miscreant to go up front and write his name on the chalkboard. You'll fill a chalkboard the width of the room in a single period and record everyone's name at least twice. Continue the ruse by having a kid copy all the names on some paper and make a big deal out of folding it ceremoniously and readying it for the principal. When the kids leave, throw it away.

Always try to keep your head turned away from the kids and remember to keep the eye closest to them slightly closed. That way, if somebody throws something at you and it hits you in the head you'll minimize any possible eye damage. Many a teacher who wasn't familiar with this ploy enjoys monocular vision as a result of his ignorance. You can spot these guys because they're all wearing eye patches and running into things on their blind side.

Oh, and forget a seating chart for study hall. It can't be done. It's humanly impossible to force 100 kids to sit in assigned seats when you don't know one from another or even if they go to your school. I know because I tried it myself years ago and almost went nuts trying to keep track of everybody.

They changed seats en masse. The same kid never sat in the same seat twice and I had no idea where the hell they belonged. I couldn't keep track of them with radar and they knew it. In no time I became the butt of their jokes and passers-by would congregate outside the study hall to watch me try to take attendance. The worst part was I had to keep up the fight all semester or admit they'd beaten me and that was the longest eighteen weeks I ever spent in my life.

Most of this is strictly for show anyway, of course. There's really no way you can effectively control a study hall in today's schools, but at least these tactics let you create the impression that you're in charge and this adds to your stature as a teacher and could even pave the way for your entry into the ranks of administrators where you'll never have to deal directly with kids again.

Of course, such an event would force you to associate with other administrators and you may well prefer dueling with the kids to such an ignominious fate.

In the meantime, be a canny observer of the scene. Note any new schemes employed by your colleagues. Swap ideas in the teachers' lounge, compare notes, innovate. Don't forget you're smarter than the kids are and you can outthink them every time if you're shrewd enough.

If all else fails fake a heart attack and have the paramedics cart you off to the sanctuary of the nearest intensive care ward for a well-earned rest.

> *If you think education is expensive,*
> *try ignorance.*
> – Derek Bok

## Chapter Two

### GIRD YOUR LOINS FOR THE PERILS OF EXTRA-CURRICULAR DUTY

Remember, survival is the name of the game. Don't lose sight of that goal as we wend our way through the maze of modern schooling in these United States. With one eye fixed firmly on that distant pension, you'll want to keep the other fixed on the kids, parents, and administrators/board members because they're the ones who can prevent your ever drawing that first check.

Survival means knowing what to expect and what worked or didn't work before. It means planning ahead and learning from the experience of colleagues and not repeating their mistakes. It means learning to bob and weave and strike unexpectedly from the flanks in your running skirmish with a loony system determined to drive you out of the building and into an asylum.

Take extra-curricular duties, for instance. There was a time when this meant overseeing an after-school dance or taking tickets for the school play or chaperoning hay rides, tame duties that were uneventful and even dull. No one was ever injured or insulted at these affairs, no one threatened or abused. Alas, such is no longer the case.

Consider an example of such a duty in these perilous

times. It's football duty at Mackenzie High in Detroit, an experience that traumatized an already jaded crew of teachers who'd experienced every outrage imaginable and were not easily alarmed.

Everybody hated football duty at the Big Mack, especially little Jimmy McAvoy in the science department. Jimmy got caught up in a stampede at one of our games a few years ago and some 250 frenzied fans trampled his inert form into the mud near the fifty-yard line. He didn't seem much the worse for wear at the time but it turned out his spirit was broken along with several vertebrae. Ever since then the poor guy has had to scamper about sideways like a sand crab with a broken hip. And Jimmy was one of the lucky ones.

My last experience on football duty is probably typical of what transpires at our average game. I was assigned the duty of collecting tickets at the gate and, incidentally, trying to thwart would-be gate crashers. In terms of danger this duty ranked somewhere between running the bulls at Pamplona and bungee jumping from a fifty-foot tower with a fifty-one foot rope.

*Survival Rule:* **Assume no dangerous duties. To avoid same, feign a limp or claim a back injury or cultivate a crazed look in your eye.**

We knew this was going to be especially tough because we were playing Preppie High, a toney, upscale-school populated largely by the sons and daughters of aristocrats who were our kids' natural enemies. Besides being a snooty school, Preppie High made the further mistake of having the best record in the city. They hadn't lost a game all year and they wouldn't lose this one without divine intervention. (We were fairly certain God wouldn't help the Mackenzie cause since that would be like Him coming to the aid of Sodom and Gomorrah.) Winning the game was our only hope, and that meant we didn't have any.

Teachers on duty were required to be there an hour before kickoff to give them a chance to prepare defensive positions and scout the terrain. Some of us would fill sandbags while others laid out bandages, tourniquets, and splints for the wounded and maimed. Stretcher-bearers were stationed at vantage points here and there to cart away casualties and a cadre of teachers armed with chair legs and garbage-can lid shields queued up behind the refreshment stand.

A few teachers were sent out as infiltrators to mingle unobtrusively with the students in an effort to learn their plans. Still, this ploy never proved fruitful because the students never made any plans; they seemed to rely on their instincts and reacted spontaneously whenever a chance to do mischief came along.

We gained comfort from the fact that we had an experienced and battle-tested crew for this game. All of us had been in the trenches long enough to have survived every possible calamity and, like tough frontline troops, we wore an air of insouciance in the quiet moments just before the battle was joined.

But it was all for show again—our terror was boundless.

I parked my car two blocks away so it wouldn't be in the line of fire in case the festivities spilled over into the surrounding streets and walked back to the field. A mob was already milling around the fence when I got there and it took me several minutes just to work my way to the gate so I could assume my post. I took some heavy elbows in the ribs and some big-footed creep walked all over my suede shoes, but I silently congratulated myself for getting in with such minor injuries.

With the gate securely chained for the moment, I decided to reconnoiter a bit to check on our defenses. I found the police massed together behind the Preppie High stands where they stood around in small groups and fidgeted nervously. Their cars were lined up in a single row and they'd taken their riot sticks from the trunks. They were taking practice swings at imaginary heads while they waited. Overhead, a police helicopter swooped low over the field and fell into a pattern of tight circles against the fall sky.

At one end of the stands a dozen Doberman pinschers, vicious, mad brutes snapped and growled menacingly and lunged against their chains in an effort to get loose and kill someone. The ugly beasts were held in ready reserve and released only as a last resort.

*Survival Rule:* **Your car is vulnerable. Never park it in the same place twice.**

The dogs weren't held out of the fray for any humanitarian reasons, though; it was mainly because they showed a profound lack of discretion in choosing targets. Once released, they were as likely to attack friend as well as foe and everybody knew it. Their principal value lay in the fact that when they entered the melee every human being, good guys and bad guys alike, vanished as if by magic and let the field go to the dogs.

I came across Marv Nussbaum sitting behind a low parapet of sandbags near the north end zone. He was basking in the warm fall sun and seemed perfectly at ease, but he was apparently not as relaxed as he looked. I approached from his blind side and I must have startled him because he suddenly whirled and struck me on top on my head with a stout stick before he recognized me.

"What the hell are you doing, Marv?" I demanded indignantly.

"Hey," he said, "I thought one of the sneaky buggers had got behind me. I'm sorry, Evan, I guess my reflexes are so finely honed now I strike without even thinking."

"Well, it's a good thing they didn't give you a gun. Nobody would be safe around you."

"I said I'm sorry."

"Yeah, well, I guess it's not really your fault. I should have been more careful myself."

I made a compress out of some Kleenex and tried to stem the flow of blood from a nasty head wound.

Marv shot nervous glances in four or five directions and continued to brandish his stick. "How do things look, Evan?" he said.

"I don't know," I said, "but my intuition tells me there's something in the air."

A soda can landed at our feet and skittered along the ground. There was a long, diabolical laugh and a chorus of voices chanting curses from behind the canvas-covered fence running along the field just past the end zone. That would be their advance guard arriving on the scene to soften us up with vicious probing attacks designed to uncover our weaknesses before they launched the main assault.

"How high do you figure the score will go?" Marv asked.

"Preppie should win by at least forty points."

"Okay, what happens if they get twenty-five points in the first quarter?"

A barrage of soda cans fell around us in a brilliant shower of reds and greens mixed with flashing silver. Marv and I dove for the sandbags. I arrived there in a dead heat with a green soda can; it caromed off my head with the most interesting "pinging" sound and raised a small welt behind my left ear.

We peeked over the parapet at the soda cans littering the landscape and Marv said, "They must have heard the question."

I decided it was time to get the hell out of there. I gave Marv the secret handshake and made my way back to the gate, pausing en route to genuflect at the little mound of grass marking the grave of Howie Harrigan, late of the foreign language department.

Howie started to come unglued right after our first uprising and went steadily downhill. He got pretty paranoid and finally took to wearing a ring of garlic around his neck to ward off evil spirits and the poor sap was beaten to death after a football game one day because he smelled so bad.

They buried him on the fifty-yard line and during each game at a special ceremony in his honor a gang of hoodlums gathers around his grave and pisses on him. It's a touching, tender ritual and the crowd never fails to respond by shouting obscenities and hurling epithets.

I got back just in time to open the gate and start letting

people in. Ed Collins, the science department head, and I followed our plan to the letter. We unchained the gate and Ed leaned his bulk against it in an effort to allow space for a single entrant at a time while I took tickets. We'd let no more than a dozen or so in when I glanced at the stands and saw they were already half-full. Students came over the fence, under it, and through it with wire-cutters; we had a nice crowd settled in and chanting for the game to begin before we knew what was going on.

Just then the crowd surged forward and the gate flew open. Ed went sprawling and hundreds of students thundered through the gate and across Ed's chest. I was knocked backward into the fence and out of harm's way as everybody rushed by and filled the stands. I helped Ed up and found him unhurt except for an oddly twisted shoulder and some scuffmarks on his face.

Talk about luck.

Let me just remark right here and now in our own defense that Ed Collins and I held that gate almost as long as Horatio held his bridge. There are those who say we broke and ran and so we did, but not until we'd both lost consciousness from wounds received. Besides, everybody knows discretion is the better part of valor and Ed and I were nothing if not discreet.

Their guerrilla training paid off for some old-timers who departed seconds before the final riot started when they surveyed the crowd with a practiced eye and instinctively sensed pending danger. Led by Ida Crocke, a cynical, one-legged old lady from the math department who hobbled about on a crutch and wanted to get a head start on them, their feet turned unbidden toward the nearest exit and they followed Ida out in a cloud of dust. This is an example of well-developed survival skills operating at warp speed, the very skills needed to make it as a teacher in these trying times.

The game only lasted until the half when Preppie was leading 56 to zip and everybody went nuts at once. Big Mack fans poured from the stands and went for the Preppie kids, their targets went for their buses, and the cops went for everybody. People were running in every direction and confusion reigned. I saw assistant-principal Bill Spanner go down under a flurry of blows and before I could go to his aid I was thrown against the fence and had an eye closed by a crisp right hand. That's when I took off.

The peanut man was worked over and deprived of his wares by a gang in the street just outside the gate. Police cars were coming from every point of the compass and the air was filled with rocks, bottles, and soda cans. As I legged it down the street a rock bounced off a parked car with a metal-crunching thud and I gave myself a mental pat on the back for having the good sense to park my car away from the scene of action.

Only the fit survive at Mackenzie High and few were fitter than I.

We had to wait until the following Monday to tally up the final score for the whole affair because we didn't know who'd turn up wounded or missing until then. It turned out that a dozen students were arrested, twenty-three injured in various degrees, and no fatalities recorded. Our side suffered no arrests, nineteen injured, no fatalities, and one missing.

Pete Bates from the auto shop was the missing teacher.

He'd been taken prisoner by a gang of insurgents and held hostage, but they only kept him three days before a settlement was negotiated. The school board agreed to give each member of the gang a fully certified high school diploma and a paid-up four year scholarship to a university of his choice. It was the least we could do for these unfortunate waifs who'd been victimized so cruelly by society. Besides, they'd have ventilated poor Pete's head if we hadn't met their terms.

So, there you have it, an accurate, truthful account of football duty at Mackenzie High School on any given Friday afternoon in the fall. It was a memorable experience, one that will stand us in good stead for many years to come, always close at hand in case we ever need material for a nightmare or the makings of a nice psychosis.

Naturally, any sensible person would like to avoid activities of this sort and that means getting out of these duties if you can. For instance, it's a good idea to report to a new school using a cane and faking a bad limp. Hint that it's a war wound, nasty shrapnel in the knee, you know. It doesn't matter whether you were actually in a war or not as nobody will question a war hero. Just get the facts straight and pick a war that you might have served in and don't claim to be a World War II vet when you're only twenty-eight years old. The same with your war story; don't forget the details or you'll end up telling different versions and be exposed as the fraud you really are.

Or pretend you're blind. Get a white cane and/or a German shepherd and claim there's nothing you'd rather do than hold back enraged fans at the next football game but, under the circumstances, etc. Only the hardest of hard-hearted principals will insist you hold back those fans.

The tricky part of this scheme is maintaining the deception throughout the year. If you use the war-wound ploy, you must remember to limp all the time. If you forget and people see you sprinting down the hall sans cane, they'll spot you as a phony and assign your devious ass to permanent lunchroom duty.

A better bet is to call in sick on football Friday and spend a relaxed day shopping or on the golf course.

*Survival Rule:* **Keep a can of pepper spray in hand while on hall duty. Spray every suspicious person who comes along, i.e., everybody.**

But if all else fails and you're faced with a duty assignment in spite of your best efforts, you need to take a close look at some of the duties found at all schools and see what you have to watch out for. Take hall duty, for example. Everybody knows what hall duty is. Teachers patrol the halls during classes to keep hall-wanderers out and intercept others who are making a break for it. This duty can be extremely dangerous, as lone teachers confronting strangers in dark hallways are taking great risks, indeed.

It used to be that the hall-duty teacher would check papers or daydream or even nod off on her post because there was nothing going on. Once in a while a solitary student would appear with a hall pass in hand on his way to the john or a colleague would stop by for a chat and it was Dullsville all the way.

Hall duty today is quite different. Once the bell rings and classes start the halls should be devoid of kids and aren't.

Late arrivals linger at their lockers and socialize with friends as though they had all day to while away. They eat food they've stored in their lockers, buy and sell mysterious packets of things unknown, laugh and dance and arrange trysts and do everything except go to class where they belong.

When the tardy crowd finally thins out the professional hall-wanderers come out of their hiding places and prowl the halls raising Cain. The hall-duty teacher is supposed to check these guys for passes and apprehend those who are found cutting class but that's not easy since these guys are always on the move and won't stop to be interrogated. In fact, that suits the teacher perfectly as the last thing you want is a confrontation with packs of outsiders who are probably armed to the teeth and have IQs of 75 or less.

So here are some tips to get you safely out of that hall in one piece. First, try for a post on the top floor, one as far away from the thugs on the ground floor as possible. There are more dangerous types on the first floor because they have to get by the cops and numerous security guards that patrol that area. As fewer thugs make it to the top floor you'll have fewer run-ins up there and appreciably increase your chances of surviving the experience.

Always sit with your back to the wall, preferably close to a classroom where a 300-pound weightlifter is teaching so when you holler for help you'll get Samson and not Delilah. Having a fire-alarm box close by is also good because if you're assaulted you can pull the alarm and have the paramedics on their way before you've even lost consciousness.

Wear shoes with rubber soles so you can run and jump

well and you may be able to out-run the thugs. Definitely avoid heels or tight skirts that restrict movement if you're a woman because you'll never be able to run fast enough or jump high enough in such garb. It's a good idea to sacrifice fashion for mobility.

If you do run into a band of rogues on hall duty put up a bold front. Don't appear timid or weak or even hesitant as this emboldens thugs who enjoy it more if their victims are helpless. Speak right up and let them know who's who, I always say.

"Hey, where do you think you're going?" you sing out when you spot those gang bangers heading your way.

"You talkin' to us?" their leader says.

"That's right, I'm talking to you. If you guys don't have hall passes, you're in big trouble. Come on, let's see 'em. Get 'em out."

Notice the authoritative tone, the crisp language without nuances that might confuse sub-marginal intellects? Plain words spoken by someone to be reckoned with, someone who's in a position of power and knows it. Most gang bangers will be intimidated and meekly follow you to the school cops to be arrested.

If the thugs you meet don't respond as expected, then this is why you're wearing those rubber soles mentioned above.

Are you asked to chaperone the school dance? This used to be a piece of cake but no longer. Most school dances are held at night and that means it's harder to see the thugs. For some reason kids who hate school worse than sin will still hang around the place as though they had no other home. School dances attract them like flies to potato salad and there's always an argument over whose property a particular girl is and the ensuing discussion is punctuated with bullets.

For some peculiar reason these bullets almost never hit their intended targets. Two gangs of thugs blasting away at each other on prom night will miss each other and shoot assorted innocent bystanders (teachers?!) every time. The bullets won't hit you, though, if you aren't there—so don't be there.

Try to get assigned to decorating the gym and you can stay home on prom night. Failing that, angle for the checkroom job; not only does that give you a place to hide when the action starts but you also might pick up some loose change with tips.

Never volunteer to chaperone senior trips or camera club outings, as you'll open yourself to lawsuits or worse. It never fails. Boys sneak into the girls' rooms and somebody produces beer and funny cigarettes and a noisy party breaks out and the management is called and the press shows up and it's scandal time all around. Solution? Never chaperone anything, especially if it's a night affair or out of town.

You can also look for special duties, the kind that don't involve supervising kids. You may edit the school paper in lieu of hall duty or compute the team's eligibility records instead of pulling football duty or work on the yearbook and skip lunchroom duty. In other words, play the angles.

Incidentally, lunchroom duty is the worst. The noise alone will do serious damage to your psyche and watching the kids eat will kill your appetite forever. In fact, dieters do well on lunchroom duty because they lose all interest in food once they're exposed to that spectacle.

Parking lot patrol is a common duty at most schools because the kids are forever stealing cars or their parts and nothing short of constant surveillance will stop them. You can expect no help from the Central Office because the kids are only stealing teachers' cars and nobody downtown gives a damn what happens to lowly teachers.

The big shots do care about themselves, though. I recall a bad period at the Big Mack when cars were being stolen at such a rate from the teachers' parking lot that some people thought we were running a Hertz agency on campus. We petitioned Central Office for a fence around our lot but they refused on the grounds of cost. A few days later, though, several cars were stolen from the Region Office's parking lot where the Grand Pooh-Bahs park and the very next day there was a rent-a-cop patrolling that lot in full uniform.

Anyway, teachers assigned this duty watch cars coming and going and check to make sure the right person is driving them. If the driver can't see over the steering wheel or the car is full of kids making merry it's stopped and all are arrested. Of course, they'll all be out that afternoon and back in the parking lot the next day but we still get a kick out of seeing them in 'cuffs and the custody of the law even if it is only for hours instead of the years they deserve.

And the game goes on. All in all, duty periods are a pain in the neck or other part of your anatomy depending on where you've been shot, stabbed, punched, kicked, or otherwise injured. Get out of it if you can, but if you can't at least avail yourself of others' experiences and play the angles.

*I am always ready to learn
although I do not always like being taught.*
– Winston Churchill

## Chapter Three

### TRICKS FOR OUT-DUELING NINTH-GRADERS

As all teachers know, when kids hit their 'teens something happens to them. They go from fresh-faced children all innocence and naiveté to cynical, sneering know-it-alls who rebel against everything and respect no one. Maybe it's rushing hormones or the side effects of acne creams but whatever it is it raises hell with teachers who have to deal with these guys.

We're talking about junior high kids and, more specifically, ninth-graders in the high school. Every teacher at Mackenzie High fears ninth-graders just as every sane person instinctively fears venomous reptiles and spiders. When I made out the new teaching schedules for the coming semester the first question everyone wanted answered was, "How many ninth-grade classes did you give me?" with none being the best answer and more than two requiring the prompt filing of a grievance with the union.

It happens that I sometimes gave a teacher new to the department, if they were strong and healthy, as many as three ninth-grade classes because it's only right that a new person be taken advantage of, but not even the heartiest and most robust teacher can deal with four classes full of these guys in a single day.

I recall one occasion when I had a former pro football player subbing in my department. He'd been forced into early retirement by a severe case of housemaid's knee after playing guard for six years in the NFL and was contemplating a career in teaching. This was his very first assignment and he was naive to say the least; he scoffed at the idea of mere kids being too tough for him to handle.

"Why," he said disdainfully, "I'm not afraid of no ninth-grade kids, not after bumpin' heads with the best linemen in the NFL for six years. You just give me the schedule and I'll show you some real teachin'."

*Survival Rule:* **Take advantage of teachers new to the school; it's only fair that they should pay their dues and, besides, if it's you or them it may as well be them.**

"Well, now," I said, "NFL linemen might be one thing, but I'm talking about our ninth-grade world history kids." I scrutinized him up and down and measured the cut of his jib, so to speak. "Have you ever been in a classroom full of these guys when they mutinied and found a dozen of them between you and the door?"

"No," he said, "but I've faced some of the toughest dudes in pro ball and never backed down yet."

"I can't talk you out of this madness?"

"Hell, no, gimme the schedule."

So I gave him the four classes. Hey, what did I know? Maybe he could do it. He certainly looked capable enough. The guy stood six-foot-six and must have weighed about 250 or so, and that would make him almost as big as some of the kids and give him a fighting chance, anyway. Besides, he asked for it.

I dropped by after his first class and inquired as to how things were going. He was still able to manage a weak smile and remarked that it was a little different than he thought it would be. After the second class he suffered some heavy heart palpitations and had a wild look in his eye, but he struggled gamely on to the third one.

I was in my office after the third class and he hurried in peering over his shoulder as though pursued by all the demons of hell. Throwing himself on his knees, he begged and pleaded with me to let him out of the fourth class claiming he was an orphan and hadn't been in his right mind when he'd agreed to take the assignment but I stood firm.

"Go on back in there before you lose your nerve," I said. "Remember, you spent six years in the NFL, you've bumped heads with the best linemen in pro ball. Hey, are you going to let a bunch of kids run you off the field?"

Whatever happened, I didn't want him chickening out on me because it would be a major blow to his self-esteem and, besides, I'd have to cover the class myself and I'd just sent my whip to the cleaners. But it wasn't any good.

He begged and pleaded some more and then got a crafty look in his eye and left, ostensibly to return to class but actually he left by the back door and was never seen in these parts again. I later heard he was working as a sponge diver in the shark-infested waters of the Caribbean and was glad to have a good job with a real future.

But none of this gives us any real insight into what makes a ninth-grader so formidable when encountered in groups larger than one. How can a class of school children wreak such havoc that strong men break and the gods avert their eyes and pretend they don't see what's going on?

*Survival Rule:* **If required to teach ninth-graders, start on Prozac at once. (And see if you can get the kids to take it, too.)**

Let's take a closer look at our average ninth-graders and see if we can find out anything about their nature and habits. For one thing, their average age is around eighteen years with the full age range running from thirteen to twenty four, depending on their early success in the public schools and the leniency of their parole officers.

The mean ninth-grader (as in vicious or average, whichever you prefer) will weigh upwards of 200 pounds and be able to knock a Clydesdale to its knees with either hand. The girls will be fully developed and comely. These "students" have an attention span of about three minutes if it's something they're really interested in like a circus, say, or a parade with clowns and crippled WWII veterans keeling over dead every block or so. As you can imagine, it's not an easy thing for the beleaguered teacher to match circuses and parades for excitement so any chance of holding a ninth-grader's attention for very long is almost nil.

They'll be tardy about forty times a semester and absent an average of twenty-five days in a term only ninety days long. (See the chapter on Hooky Players.) It's considered a loss of face to appear in class with your textbooks and supplies and it's a tragic social error to pass a test with a score any higher than the lowest possible passing grade required. Anyone so ill bred as to be a good student is made a laughingstock and is pelted with spitballs and jibes and sometimes gets the crap kicked out of him.

*Survival Rule:* **Be subtle and they'll never know what the hell you're up to.**

Anyway, let me tell you how it was when I had to cover one of these classes for a teacher in my department who showed the white feather and went home early one day just because some hooligans smashed four of her fingers in a door. Our own surgeon was willing to operate right here in our school clinic but the teacher petulantly insisted on a doctor who was sober.

Relying on my guerrilla training with its emphasis on surprise, I didn't go to the classroom until a minute or two after the bell because if I arrived any earlier the kids would see they had a sub and they'd split to roam the halls starting fires and riots. Instead, I skulked around a corner and waited for a chance to catch them unawares; then I rushed them before they could rally their forces. Two or three always got away, of course, but what the hell you only do what you can.

Once in the room the first job is to get them into seats and try to establish a little order and that's not easy to do because they're standing on windowsills and desktops, rummaging through the teacher's desk drawers, writing obscenities on the chalkboard, throwing lighted matches at one another, dancing, shredding textbooks, and generally high on a crazy anarchy trip.

In addition to striking real fear into your heart, it's also the moment of truth for the teacher because the next seconds will decide your fate in this situation. Ninth-graders can sense weakness and indecision the moment either makes an appearance and it brings out the bloodlust in them. You have to assert yourself right from the start and let them know who's going to run things in that room.

For example, on the day in question I used my hide-around-the-corner trick and took them by surprise, trapping all of them in the room except one speedy little devil who oozed through my outstretched arms like eighty-five pounds of quicksilver pouring down a flight of stairs.

Inside, an insane babble mixed with outraged cries.

"What?!" a kid in a red hat demanded. "Ain't Ms. Johnson here?"

"Hey, man, we got a sub!" another said.

"Say what?!"

"What happened to Ms. Johnson, man?" another shouted.

"Okay," I said, going into my act, "let's get in those seats. Put that chair down, Slick, and sit in it."

"He called you Slick, Louie."

Louie frowned.

"All you guys there," I said, "get down off the windowsills. Don't you know if somebody falls out of the window I'll have to make out a report? Christ, I've got enough paperwork to do already."

A fat kid snatched a tall, skinny kid's hat off and tossed it out of the window.

"What'd you do that for?" the skinny kid said.

*Survival Rule:* **Studies show that a smiling teacher is regarded as weak so scowl a lot.**

The fat kid laughed and the other guy hit him with a sneaky right cross before the hittee could rise from his chair. I bounded over to the window and broke up the ensuing fight by pointing a finger at each fighter and threatening permanent expulsion to the next guy who threw a punch. Gazing quickly around, I called on all my many years' experience in the trenches making crucial character judgments and chose a lad I knew instinctively could be trusted.

"Hey, pal" I said, "run down and get that hat for me, will you? I'll tell Ms. Johnson to give you an 'A' for the day."

He grinned and scampered out and the skinny kid took up his post at the window to oversee the retrieval of his property.

I'd no sooner got my record book back from a kid who was sitting at the teacher's desk laboriously changing all his grades written in blue ink to higher scores with a red ballpoint pen when a cry from the window drew my attention.

"Hey, teacher, he's stealin' my hat!"

I peered through the window to see the unscrupulous thief sprinting off down the sidewalk, the grin still on his mug and waving his newly acquired hat in the air. I looked at the skinny kid and shrugged. What the hell did I know?

*Survival Rule:* **Don't trust the kids, especially the ones who look most trustworthy.**

I managed to get some semblance of order and began taking the roll.

"Rogers, Benny," I called out.

No answer.

"Ben Rogers?" I called again.

"There go Benny," a kid in the third row said, pointing to another guy sitting five rows away from his assigned seat.

"All right, Benny," I said, "get over here in your own seat."

"I'm in my own seat," Benny said.

"Not according to this chart, you're not. Ms. Johnson has you marked on the seating chart as sitting in this seat right here and that's where you're going to sit."

"But Ms. Johnson move me here, didn't she, Juan?"

"Yeah," Juan lied.

"Benny," I said, "I don't care if the governor moved you to that seat, the chart says you sit here and I don't want to discuss it any further. Now move or I'll come back there and grab hold of you and turn you every way but loose."

This last statement produced a tense moment or two while everybody tried to figure out what was happening. They looked at Benny and back at me and a few started to laugh because it was obvious I wasn't really going back there and do anything to Benny, a young man weighing in at 200 pounds and possessed of fifteen-inch forearms. Even Benny laughed and I knew I was in the clear.

"Okay, man," he said, getting up, "I'll sit there but you're puttin' me in the wrong seat."

"Okay, Benny, that's cool. Where's Carmelita Juarez?"

"She quit," a girl in the first row said. "She's pregnant."

"Oh, pregnant, eh? Okay, we'll check her off. Where's Agnes Sosnowski?"

And so it went. Everybody played musical chairs while the attendance was being taken and I never knew whether

I'd already marked somebody present or absent or even if he belonged in the class at all. I erased and crossed out names and added others until the record book looked like Jesse James' scratchpad and I finally quit in disgust. Almost twenty minutes squandered trying to take attendance and we hadn't even peeked into the Middle Ages yet.

I searched around and located Ms. Johnson's sub plans. She had written the following:

Sixth-hour world history, room 322. Have class write answers to questions 1 thru 6 p. 243. Collect papers at end of the period. If class finishes early, go over answers orally.
(They won't finish early.)

Special notes: Don't let Elroy go to the lavatory, as he pisses on the radiator and the custodian gets mad. Watch Billy, he sits by the door, because he'll sneak out when you aren't looking.
(I looked for Billy and found he'd already departed.)

Keep an eye on Wendy and Thelma, they're vicious little agitators. Don't upset Henry, he's on parole for manslaughter and has a short fuse. First aid stuff's in the closet. Have a nice day.

I found a girl who knew how to write and had her put the assignment on the chalkboard while I watched the class for any signs of unrest.

Incidentally, I never write on the chalkboard with ninth-graders in the room because that would mean turning my back on them and no experienced veteran of the public school wars would ever commit so glaring a blunder.

Those who had books opened them to randomly selected pages and people began circulating around the room while they borrowed and loaned sheets of paper to write on and something to write with, all parties carrying on a lively conversation all the while.

"I need a pencil."

"Here go a pencil. Who got some paper?"

"How much you want for that weed?"

"Hey, quit steppin' on my shoe, man!"

"I'll step on your head if you don't shut up!"

"What page we on, Jose?"

"Who cares, man? Them pages is all the same, man."

After several minutes of this everybody got more or less back to his seat and the lesson began in earnest. Five or six kids put their heads down on their desks and fell asleep as though drugged, long since having learned that this was the only sensible way to cope with world history. Four kids in a corner turned their desks around to form a playing surface and commenced their usual afternoon game of whist while two or three kibitzers watched attentively.

Rock music poured from a radio hidden somewhere in the room and a little guy in the back kept time with the music by stabbing a pocketknife into the desktop. The noise level in the room fell off until the decibel range was somewhere between a medium-sized foundry and a Baptist revival meeting deep in the Bible Belt, about par for an average ninth-grade classroom in Mackenzie High.

I passed the remaining time struggling to stay on top of things as best I could. Darting about the room in a frenzy I put the card players out of business and turned my attention to the task of driving the loungers away from the window where they'd congregated to hurl oaths and challenges at passers-by. I'd no sooner managed to beat them back from the window with the aid of a chair leg than I had to rout the card players again because they'd resumed their game the moment my attention was diverted by the crowd at the window. Meanwhile, I kept an ear cocked to try to track down the hidden radio (I never did find the damn thing) and on two occasions I had to go to the door to repel invasions by angry mobs of hall-wanderers.

With five minutes to go in the period I'd already broken up three card games, interceded in two fights and driven off two all-out attacks by outsiders, put down a major mutiny and nipped another one in the bud, cleared the riffraff from the windows six times, dispatched a brace of thugs to their counselors for "guidance", i.e., electric shock treatments, summoned our security forces to haul Henry the Manslaughter Kid away when he went berserk because I wouldn't let him pound little Phil Jordan into a pulp, and had to call the custodian with his mop after I refused to give Elroy a pass to the lavatory and the clown pissed all over the floor.

*Survival Rule:* **Cultivate the custodian. Not only is he invariably smarter than the principal but he'll prove more useful, too.**

I was applying a tourniquet to my arm to stop the flow of blood from a nasty bite inflicted by Wanda Sims when I took her cigarettes away because she insisted on smoking in the room when somebody pulled a fire alarm and the place exploded with bits and pieces of ninth-graders disintegrating all over the landscape.

I tried to form them up in a line to evacuate the building but it was like trying to corral a roomful of cats after a hundred-pound mastiff had been thrown into their midst. The kids thundered from the room and raced off in every direction and I sneaked back to my office in the confusion to tend my wounds and roundly curse Ms. Johnson for going home early.

So now you can see why we all fear ninth-grade students at Mackenzie High and why you'll want to avoid contact with the species if at all possible. If you do end up facing a roomful of these guys, reread this chapter and memorize its rules and you'll have at least a 50/50 chance of coming out of the experience with a whole skin.

As it stands now, though, ninth-graders all over America are swiftly driving each of us to an early retirement, an early grave, or the home for mental defectives and twisted pedagogues.

Don't you be one of them.

*If a boy be of a mischievous, wicked inclination, no school will ever make him good.*
– Henry Fielding

## Chapter Four

### HOW TO FOIL HOOKY PLAYERS

Be ever watchful that your mind doesn't begin to slip from dealing with the insanity that surrounds you every day. Inane policies from the super, unworkable plans, constant failure can all influence your mental and even physical health. When forced to take part in madness, it's easy to go mad yourself.

Our struggle against the hooky players, for example, drove several members of our staff over the brink and they remain there to this day. We first began to suspect that we had an attendance problem at Mackenzie High when someone noticed early one morning that we were running about nine kids per class during first hour. If nothing else, you would think we'd notice the ominous silence. Our principal, Dr. Homer Fluker, called a meeting of his department heads for that very afternoon to deal with the problem.

We met in the teachers' lunchroom, our regular meeting place. It was also a resort area for half-a-million cockroaches and assorted other vermin that were waging a guerrilla war of their own with us as the opposition. Our meetings were punctuated with the slapping sounds made by size-twelve brogans crushing the little brown beggars to death on the tile floor. Scores of bodies would litter the place after a meeting and the tiny, heart-rending cries of the wounded would sound in our ears as we filed from the room with our feet flying like so many broken caricatures of Bojangles, stomping roaches as we went.

"Well," Fluker said, striking to the heart of the matter even as Alexander assailed the Gordian Knot, "we seem to have a little problem here. Does anybody know what it is?"

The answers came from all quarters.

"Too many thugs in the halls!"

"Not enough security!"

"Unsanitary conditions!"

This last suggestion was followed by a salvo of shoe leather striking the floor and the anguished death cries of dozens of scurrying roaches.

"Teachers' cars being stolen from the parking lot!"

"Drugs in school!"

"Unbridled sex!" This comment came from Jack Ryan from math. Jack had had a little trouble adjusting to the sexual revolution of recent times and tended to see evil everywhere he looked. Of course, he'd have seen a whole lot less evil if he hadn't spent so much time trying to see up the girls' miniskirts.

"No, no, no," Fluker said impatiently, "I mean a new problem. We've already studied all those other things."

Assistant principal Bill Spanner, the guy in charge of discipline (his only duty, it took all of his time), was sitting to one side of Fluker and he took a magic marker and spelled out "attendance" [sic] on the back of a big manila envelope.

He held it up and we all said it at once.

"Attendance!"

Fluker blinked. "Of course," he said uncertainly, "attendance." He collected his wit—he only had one—and went on. "We seem to be running out of kids around here. Nobody comes to school anymore."

*Survival Rule:* **Avoid all committees. There is no uglier sight than people who are trying to think in unison.**

"Say, that's right," Sam Browne from the vocational department said as he adjusted his belt, "I've noticed it myself. We've got more kids hangin' around the flagpole than we have in the building lately."

"That's what I mean," Fluker said, "our absentee rate is getting higher than some of the kids and we've got to put a stop to it. Now, I'm open to suggestions, let's come up with a plan to solve this attendance problem for good and all."

In the awkward silence that followed we could hear the muted commands of the roach leaders as they formed up their ranks for another go at us. At last, Coach Bixby broke the ice.

"The law says they got to be in school so let's call the cops and have them arrested for truancy," he said.

"Expel them!" somebody called out.

"Get a federal grant and pay them for coming to school!"

"Use attendance as a basis for all grades and pass the kids who come to class regularly. Fail everybody else."

"Use peer pressure. Get some jocks to beat the crap out of anybody who cuts class!"

"Threaten them! Tell them if attendance doesn't improve, we'll close down all the johns and hundreds will be homeless!"

And so on. Each suggestion was carefully noted and discussed before it was discarded as utterly worthless. The meeting was rapidly degenerating into our usual exercise in futility until Ed Collins suggested we call in the Region attendance people and let them do the job they were supposed to be doing. This plan was widely approved by all hands as a viable solution in spite of the fact that it meant admitting to the Region Office that we had a problem we couldn't handle.

A joint committee was set up between the Region attendance department and Mackenzie High with each side furnishing eight members. Some of our most unlikely students suddenly developed a strong sense of school spirit and volunteered to serve on the committee, but they quit in disgust after the first meeting when they discovered we were studying attendance rather than joints.

A series of meetings was scheduled over a three-month period with a deadline for final recommendations at the end of the ninety days. The committee was charged with a single goal: get the kids back into their classes and use any means, fair or foul, to get the job done.

Of course, the committee never met the deadline because we were never able to muster enough members at one time to constitute a quorum. It seems the committee on truancy would have done well to put its own house in order before trying to reform others. The committee never did get a quorum so nothing ever came of it and eventually everybody forgot about the whole thing and the truants laughed at us—again.

Does this mean we're helpless, then? Isn't there something we can do to fight back? Of course there is. After all, we're college graduates, for God's sake. We're smarter than they are, aren't we? I've outlined certain ideas that will help even the odds in the ongoing struggle between us and offer them below for your consideration.

For openers, we all know every normal American kid plays hooky at least once in a while; in fact, I have no use for a kid with a perfect attendance record. I always figure the guy is up to no good and keep a close watch on him to make sure he doesn't do anything irregular.

It's true. Perfect attendance isn't normal behavior anywhere. The kid who comes in with a shotgun and decimates his English class one day is always the same kid who goes to church four or five times a week, is an Eagle Scout, and has perfect attendance since kindergarten. Never trust such people.

Fortunately, such kids are rare, indeed. The large majority of high school kids today play hooky every chance they get and, accordingly, quickly become skilled pros in deception and outright lying. As their teacher, it's your duty to see that these guys don't make a monkey of you by fooling you with their bag of hooky-player tricks.

And what, exactly, are some of these tricks aimed at making you look like a monkey? Following are some of the more devious ones that I encountered personally, and remember that I was up against world-class hooky players at the Big Mack.

For example, always be especially alert when you are yourself returning to school after playing hooky for a day or so. The kids who skipped the same days you did always check to see if you were absent before they reveal they weren't there. If they learn you were absent too the charlatans will claim they were there and the sub must have made a mistake. They'll call on a friend for corroboration and he'll lie through his teeth to back up his pal. The game here is to raise some uncertainty in your mind and force you to give the guy the benefit of the doubt. Refuse to be gulled. Consider the sub's records infallible. Treat the absence as genuine and insist on a certified absence excuse regardless of how many liars the kid produces as witnesses. Never waver in your resolve or you'll look like that monkey and so will your colleagues.

Another dodge that works for a lot of kids is just to claim they forgot their excuse but they promise to bring it tomorrow for sure. The plan here is to stall as long as possible and hope you'll get tired of asking for it or finally forget it altogether.

*Survival Rule:* **Don't forget, kids mean jobs. Fake the numbers; count them there when they're not. Carry no-shows forever.**

So don't forget. Mark it down in big letters. Demand that note or else. If it isn't in your hands within two days get on the phone and call home. Show them you're nobody's fool, by God.

And watch out for the kid who'll steal your seating charts if left unattended. He'll erase his name from the thing and never appear again and you'll never know he's missing. Don't leave seating charts lying around where they can be purloined and altered.

Never send absence notices home in the mail. Most kids can recognize an official school envelope with a single glance and they'll intercept the things and burn them around ceremonial fires at midnight. A recent government study showed that a mere 3% of official school envelopes ever reach a parent, and it only happens in these cases because the kid was unable to read well enough to identify the official seal.

Use the phone to notify parents of truancy. Even then you can't always be sure of whom you're really talking to since the clever rascals will have friends pretend to be their parent. You can easily trip them up in cases where you suspect this is going on by innocently asking the "parent" for the kid's middle name or birth date or something similar that mom would know and the kid's half-witted friend wouldn't.

An area of special concern has to do with absence excuses. The little devils are ingenious beyond belief and will devise schemes that would trick Holmes and Watson both. For example, I knew several kids who used the Phony Christian ploy and hoodwinked half the school before they were finally exposed as imps from hell and given their just deserts.

In this gambit, the kid learns which teachers have a religious bent and cons them into believing he's one of them by carrying a Bible around with him, one of those thirty-pound jobs with colored ribbons hanging out of all the places he's marked for memorizing, and he shows up sans note after a ten day absence with a phony cast on his arm. He tells the teacher he fell off a ladder while helping the deacon paint the church, a story no good Christian would challenge under the circumstances.

Moral: Get that deacon on the phone and nail this guy.

What about absence notes? This is where the cleverer ones really shine. A good excuse shows boldness. A phone number is included to lend an air of authenticity to the fraud. After all, would a guilt-ridden hooky player have the balls to dangle that tempting phone number right in front of the teacher's nose like that?

Damn right he would, especially if he's a pro who makes his living skipping school. This is the kid who's out more than he's in, the guy whose name you never learn because you don't see him often enough to find out who the hell he is.

We have whole schools full of these guys in Detroit. They're real pros, the best in the business. Most of them can't read a whole sentence in a row without getting lost, but you'd swear they were all Harvard law graduates when you try to hang a truancy rap on them. They're familiar with every existing law on the books dealing with truancy and they make up new ones as they go along.

They know all the nuances of the game and employ their own guerrilla tactics. Instead of claiming their grandmother died (a real cliché in the absence excuse trade) they'll claim the whole family was wiped out and they had to attend funerals in four different states and that's why they haven't been in school for the past month.

These guys always include a phone number in the note but it's always a phony number. They never live where the records say they do, either. In fact, a lot of them are actually nomads and have no real homes that you can find anywhere. And they write absence notes that would fool P. T. Barnum himself.

Consider this example of such a note written by a pro.

This is a verbatim copy of one received by Marv just the other day.

> Dear Mr. Nussbaum:      10-21
> Please excuse Billy's absence yesterday.
> He had a dental appointment.
> Please call me at 555-1212 if there
> are any questions.
>                    Mrs. Jane Smith

There, short and to the point. Nothing subtle about it even as it teems with subtle overtones. I'd readily accept this note myself—and have a thousand times. It's perfect. Observe the direct challenge for the teacher to call, almost daring her to call. A masterful touch.

There's really no defense against the pros; they're too good, anybody can be could be taken in by these guys. The only caveat I can offer is to know they're out there and suspect everything.

Just to illustrate how brilliant these kids can be, here's another example of a note I received from one who could teach grad courses on the subject.

> Dr. Keliher:       2-14
> Jack was absent yesterday because our
> house burned down. He stayed home to help
> us look thru the ashes for our furniture.
> You can call me at my sister's house
> where we're staying. 555-1212
>                    Mrs. Jane Smith

Nicely done, but the real beauty of this note lies in the fact that it was written on the back of an old envelope that was actually water marked and singed around the edges! I knew the note was a phony at once, of course, but I accepted it immediately as a tribute to the skill of a master craftsman and gave the crooked little schemer a clean bill of health for the entire month. I believe in rewarding excellence wherever I find it.

As you can see, there's much at stake in this little game. It's them against you, mind versus mind, wits matching wits. If you aren't on your toes and quick, you'll be that monkey and scorned by all as a fool and numbskull or worse.

So be alert. Analyze those notes. Make those calls. Grill them. Verify everything. Show them they can't out-fox you, by God.

*A young man who is not a radical about something
is a pretty poor risk for education.*
— Jacques Barzun

## Chapter Five

### SUMMER SCHOOL AND DANTE'S INFERNO

Since we're talking about survival let's remark on still another horror you may find yourself in if you aren't careful. Yes, the much-feared summer school, an experience to be avoided at all costs.

Everybody hates it. The kids hate it because it's always hotter than hell and boring beyond belief. The teachers hate it for the same reasons. Scientists say time can actually slow down; any teacher who's ever taught summer school would tell them it can come to a dead stop.

***Survival Rule:*** **Do not teach summer school. Do not teach summer school. Do not... Well, you get the idea.**

There's something exceedingly depressing about the whole thing. Summer school is an aberration. If God had meant for teachers to waste away in summer school, He'd have at least air-conditioned the buildings. As it is, it's like being sentenced to a term in hell for some nameless peccadillo in some other life somewhere.

In the first place, summer school is a place for losers, the guys who couldn't deal with "regular" school and end up going to school in July as a result. Visit your average summer school class and you'll find the place is full of hooky players and jocks and bikers and dropouts and similar riffraff. Needless to say, these are the very people you'd most like to avoid, and you can do that by staying the hell out of summer school.

There are also some science club types in summer school. These people actually like it because they don't know anything about playing baseball or hanging out on street corners or getting laid, all factors that make them losers in their own right and people you want to avoid as much as the biker/jock/reefer salesman crowd.

As a rule, only extreme poverty will motivate a teacher to sign on for the summer. They regard it as a trial and an ultimate sham. If the kids attend regularly and can drag themselves through the interminable hour-and-a-half long classes in 90* heat, they feel they're automatically entitled to a passing grade. Any "work" that goes on is incidental and totally unexpected. Everybody just wants to get it over with.

It happened one summer that I was tapped out and was unable to get my usual summer job as a carnival roustabout and had to take a summer school job. The temperature on the first day was 91* and I found my class bathed in sweat and already bored stiff. I surveyed the assemblage with a practiced eye and recognized most of them as recidivists who went to summer school every year because they never learned to stay the hell out of the place.

"Okay, this is a civics class," I said. "If you're in the wrong class now's the time to find it out." (As always, three or four people got up and left. More would leave later when they discovered they were also in the wrong class.) "Take out your civics books and open them to the first chapter. Read that chapter. When you finish, answer the questions at the end. Any questions?"

People groaned aloud, great sighs issued forth, despair settled over all. As soon as everyone was engaged, I ducked out and went down the hall for a cold soda and met fifteen fellow guerrillas gathered at the cold drink machine and we spent the next half-hour cursing our woeful karma and planning counterattacks. We would spend many hours so engaged.

Everybody swelters in summer school. The chief concern is keeping cool and that means staying outside the classroom as much as possible. Twenty or thirty perspiring bodies can give off the heat of a moderate-sized blast furnace so get out when you can. If you're on the first floor, stand outside and lean in the window. Drink lots of cold drinks but don't let the kids see you, as it will only add to their anguish.

If there's a fan point it at your desk and assure everyone that the air currents in the room require the fan to move the air toward you for maximum efficiency—no matter where you sit. Wet paper towels and press them against your brow. Don't let the kids do this, though, as they'll end up throwing them against the ceiling because that's what they do with wet towels.

At frequent intervals announce that you have some pressing business down the hall and will be right back. Then scoot out to the parking lot and turn on the air in your car and take a twenty-minute break to cool down.

Count the kids every half-hour. Summer school is so awful most kids can't take it too long without a break and a few more sneak out every time you turn your back. It isn't unusual to start with twenty-five kids and end up with a four-person seminar by lunch.

Finally, pass everyone. The kids are right; anybody who sits through summer school deserves to pass and should. Besides, it's dangerous to flunk a guy who's sweated through eight weeks of hell only to fail in the end. Such a guy often reacts unreasonably and tends to focus responsibility for his troubles on your maligned ass. It's not worth it; pass the guy and spare yourself the hassle.

As I said, it's a bad deal. Instead of summer school, see if you can't float a loan or sell some spare body parts or hijack a truck or something. Anything. Just skip that particular level of hell if at all possible.

*'Tis education that forms the common mind;
just as the twig is bent, the tree's inclined.*
– Alexander Pope

## Chapter Six

### YOU AND GOD

Tampering with things religious in the public schools is a good way to end up in court or even dead. The religious-right wackos will sue you if you don't and the atheists will do the same if you do. Introduce religion and the Muslim Jihad people will send someone over to shoot the principal, the Hottentots will demand equal time, evangelists will show up with a truckload of tracts and you'll never know a sane moment again.

Knowing all that we made it a practice to proceed with caution in this regard. If the Christians hadn't murdered her Madalyn Murray O'Hair would be pleased to hear that Mackenzie High School is closely following the guidelines set down by the Supreme Court when it comes to the teaching of religion in the public schools. (Indeed, not only do we refrain from teaching religion in our schools but, in order to avoid the possibility of breaking any other laws we don't even know about, we don't teach anything else, either.)

While it's true there may be isolated cases of unauthorized prayer in our school as, for example, when some unfortunate is in the process of being robbed and manhandled by an unruly mob, in general we scrupulously adhere to a no religion policy.

I think it's even fair to say you will search the world over before you find another group more zealous in avoiding anything to do with religion than our own faculty and administration. We've long since learned that God is helpless to do anything about our situation and nobody wants to embarrass Him by applying for aid we know He can't deliver. Even God has limitations, you know.

*Survival Rule:* **Go ahead, break the law and pray in school. It won't help but give it a try, anyway.**

We often wandered into the field of religion during the course of class discussions on various subjects and the knowledge some students displayed of the Bible and the Christian faith is something astonishing to behold.

For instance, one day I wanted to show my class that I was as trapped by the rules as they were and I said, "I'm as powerless to do anything about this business as Pontius Pilate was to do anything for Christ."

A kid in a baseball cap said, "Who's he?"

"Who was Pontius Pilate?"

"No, man, this Christ dude."

"Hey," Andy Zaleski said, "you know him, Malcolm. He's that Mexican kid used to go here."

"Come on, now," I said, "you guys know all about Jesus Christ, for Christ's sake. You went to Sunday school when you were little and they must have told you about Jesus."

"Yeah," Carlos said, "he's the guy whose mama was a virgin."

"Say what?"

"Yeah, ain't that right, Dr. Keliher?"

"That's what they say, Carlos. His mother was a virgin."

"Ain't this some shit?" Malcolm said in disgust. "Ain't no man can have a mama who's a virgin."

"Well, this one did," I said.

"Yeah?" Malcolm said, ever the infidel. "How'd she get pregnant, then?"

Glancing around the room, I realized it wasn't going as well as I'd hoped in the beginning, but I was in for it now and there wasn't anything to do but forge ahead.

"Uh, I think God made her pregnant," I said.

"How did he do it?" Malcolm asked.

"They didn't say."

"Did her husband be there when God make her pregnant?"

"No."

"How do he know God do it?"

"She told him."

"Now, jus' a minute here," Malcolm said, fixing me with a steely stare. "This lady's a virgin when she marry this dude an' she's pregnant so she tell her husband God's the one who make her pregnant?"

"That's how it went," I said.

"An' he believe that?!"

"Of course."

Everybody laughed then and gave each other high fives and commented on poor Joseph's gullibility. I changed the subject and moved on to a consideration of vertical and horizontal expansion of cities. We'd had enough religious training for the moment.

As you can see, it's hopeless. None of the kids gives a damn about prayers and religion in schools; most of them haven't even got the faintest idea of what religion they are and almost none of them knows anything at all about his professed faith. The whole business is an issue with do-gooders and vested interests only and a sure pain in the neck for any teacher who gets involved on any level.

As with drugs, just say no.

> *The business of the American teacher is to liberate American citizens to think apart and act together.*
> – Stephen B. Wise

## Chapter Seven

### SAVOR LITTLE VICTORIES FOR YOU HEALTH'S SAKE

Little by little they eat away at us until we're entirely bereft of even a semblance of control or authority. For example, consider Ida's run-in with a guy in the hall one day.

Ida was in a foul mood already since someone had stolen her crutch and forced her to improvise with a broomstick while a new custom crutch was made up. She was hobbling along the hallway on her jury-rigged leg when she spotted a kid at his locker. Always the dedicated one, she stopped and accosted him.

"Hey! Have you got a hall pass?"

"Yeah," the kid said, holding up a slip of paper.

"Here, let me see that!" She snatched the paper and read it. "This isn't a hall pass!"

"Say what?" the kid said, feigning innocence.

"This is an overdue book notice from the library. No hall pass, overdue books out, that does it, pal. I'm runnin' you in. Give me your ID card."

"What you want it for?" the kid said belligerently.

Ida was outraged. "What do I want it for?!" She danced about swinging her broomstick around her head menacingly. "Why, if you don't give me that ID card right now, I'll wrap this crutch around your skinny neck...!"

Several idlers drifted up and stood around watching events unfold. While Ida was belaboring the kid about his failure to have a legal pass a band of student guerrillas arrived on the scene carrying crowbars and commenced breaking into some lockers in the background. As Ida hassled the kid at the locker, the locker thieves tried on hats and coats and stuffed booty in their pockets.

"That ain't no crutch, lady," the kid said disdainfully. "That's only a broomstick."

The loitering kids nearby laughed and that infuriated Ida even more. She was about to fly into an uncontrollable rage and flail the crap out of everybody in sight with her broomstick when I rounded the corner and interceded.

"Okay, Ida," I said, "what's going on here? This guy giving you some trouble?"

The kids in the background popped open another locker and distributed the swag.

"This guy has no hall pass and he refuses to give me his ID card!" she ranted.

"Oh, is that so?" I said. "Okay, buddy, let's..."

"Be careful!" Ida warned. "He's also got overdue library books out!"

On hearing this, I drew back and gave the guy more room. "Overdue books, eh? Okay, hand over that ID card before I call the cops and have them haul you down to the station."

The kid began rummaging through his pockets and fished out his ID card. "Oh, you want my ID card? Why didn't you say so? I got it right here." He handed it over and pulled a slip of paper from his other pocket at the same time. "An' here go my hall pass, too. It was right here all the time. How you suppose that happened?"

"Let me see that!" Ida snapped, as she grabbed the pass and inspected it. "Why, you no good...! You had it all the time! Why, I ought a...!" Ida raised her broomstick and advanced on the kid. I sprang in and grappled with her.

"Don't hit him, Ida! You know we're not allowed to hit the students!"

"What student!" she demanded, struggling to get at him. "Who wants to hit a student? I want to hit that jackass over there!"

"Okay, buddy," I said, forcibly restraining Ida, "get your stuff and beat it. Next time somebody asks you for a hall pass hand the damn thing over!"

The kid closed his locker and sauntered off while I calmed Ida down.

"Don't let them get you down, Ida," I said. "It's all part of a plot; they're trying to drive us crazy."

***Survival Rule:* A caveat: some of them are smarter than they look.**

Well, Ida was still pissed. She broke away and commenced dancing wildly about and menacing one and all with her broomstick.

"What do you mean they're trying to drive us crazy?! Everybody in this place is already crazy! You have to be crazy to be in this place! This is a crazy place! It's a place for crazy people! Craziness is the password here! Why, if you want crazy, I'll give you crazy...!"

Ida started to foam at the mouth and her eyes crossed. I was worried about her. I thought maybe she'd gone over the edge so I hauled off and belted her one to snap her out of it. She staggered under the blow and put a hand to her jaw. Her eyes uncrossed, she came to her senses, and repeated the immortal line from every B-movie ever made.

"Thanks, Evan. I needed that."

"Forget it, Ida," I said. "You'd do the same for me." I looked around smugly and gave my lapels a tug. "Well, anyway, we struck another blow for law and order, didn't we? Nobody gets away with anything when we're on the job."

"Yeah," Ida agreed, "nobody pulls the wool over our eyes!"

We nodded resolutely to each other and strode off firm in the knowledge that we'd just made another major contribution to the well being of mankind everywhere. The locker thieves left a half-dozen broken lockers in their wake and headed in the opposite direction with their arms full of booty. I figured at least it was a draw.

Your lesson: For God's sake, settle for a draw anytime you can get one and be thankful things turned out so well.

*The aim of a college education is to teach you to know a good man when you see one.*
– William James

## Chapter Eight

### THWARTING SNOOPERVISORS

If the administration is on its toes—not a safe assumption by any means—you will be observed from time to time by your superiors in order to evaluate your performance. Most teachers find this a trying experience, especially since the person doing the evaluating isn't half the teacher the observed is and they both know it. It's important that you be able to finesse these guys because a bad report can complicate your life no end.

Supervisors use all sorts of approaches to these observations. I knew one guy who slid forms under each teacher's door and had them fill out their own evaluation. Some people observe by lurking outside classroom doors and eavesdropping. Others stop by and pretend they have some other business there and then surreptitiously scout the place for signs that all is not well.

I've even known principals that listen to the classroom PA system on the sly, a devious and thoroughly dishonest practice, I might add. Most, though, are up front about it and come in and plop down and watch you teach and these are the guys you need to learn to deal with.

Here are some tricks to give you the upper hand. First, remember your training and hit them where they're weakest by scheduling an appointment so you decide which class he sees. If he observes your second-hour class, the one with Knuckles Brannigan and One-Eyed Martinez in it, you're a goner. Better he sees your fourth-hour class with all those honors kids in it. At least most of them can read and aren't on parole.

Next, keep an empty seat near the window where the warm afternoon sun pours in and induces drowsiness in whoever sits there. Hide a small radio nearby and play barely audible lullabies in a kind of auditory subliminal message. With any luck the old fool will fall fast asleep and slumber through the entire lesson and you'll be home free.

Naturally, he'll want to see your lesson plans so plan ahead. During your first year of teaching draw up plans that bristle with goals and objectives and outcome-based bullshit. Spell everything out, draw arrows this way and that, underline stuff and include footnotes. Add as much jargon as you can to confuse them should anyone actually read the thing. Try to make them even more boring than they already are and don't date them.

If done properly you need never concern yourself with lesson plans again. Always have that original plan book handy for snoopers and you can keep a year's worth of your real plans on a 4x6 index card as all the other teachers do.

*Survival Rule:* **When being observed by your supervisor, fake it. Use fake plans, fake the lesson, fake the guy out. It's all a lot of crap, anyway.**

Now for the best part. Offer the kids a 10% boost in their grades (that'll get some of them all the way up to 50%) to conspire with you to hoodwink the supervisor even further. Have a prearranged lesson ready for this moment. Give each kid a worksheet complete with questions and rehearsed answers. As soon as the guy walks in you settle him comfortably in that warm sunlight, give those incredibly boring lesson plans the slip, the kids whip out those worksheets, you start the lullabies and go into your phony spiel.

"Now, class, we'll continue yesterday's discussion of world geography," you say, ignoring the fact that there was a full-scale riot yesterday that had nothing to do with world geography. "Who can name an important South American desert?" All hands shoot skyward and you call on Billy.

"The Atacama Desert," Billy says proudly.

"That's right!" you declare. "And who knows its annual rainfall? Rita?"

"Two point four inches and no rain ever falls in some parts," Rita says.

"And what country owns it? Jackie?"

"Chile but they took it away from Bolivia in a war."

And so on. Follow up with some phony board work and split them into groups and have them color in outline maps of Australia, and all of it rehearsed like a Broadway play. Your students come across as whiz kids and you look like you know what the hell you're doing and it's all a set-up. That's what I call lesson planning like a pro, by God.

When the supervisor leaves caution the kids not to break out in loud guffaws as this might make him think something's up and you don't want to encourage thinking in an administrator if you can help it.

A still better plan is to snoop around a bit yourself and

see if you can get the goods on your supervisor and blackmail him to give you glowing reports without ever entering your room. Is he carrying on a dalliance with the girls' swimming coach? Try to get photos. Does he turn in all the marijuana he confiscates from the kids or is he holding some back for his own stash? See if you can sneak some of his urine and have the stuff analyzed; if there's pot in there you're home free.

In any case, the usual advice applies. Play the angles, bob and weave, never let them know what you're thinking—or even that you are thinking.

*Who dares to teach must never cease to learn.*
– John C. Dana

## Chapter Nine

### SURVIVING THE DREADED TEACHERS' MEETING

Principals regularly call teacher meetings after school because they look good in the monthly report. Lots of meetings indicate he's on top of things and that he knows what's going on. Of course, no one ever evaluates these affairs to see what they're about or if anything meaningful takes place at them; their appearance in the report is all that's required.

The reason you need a separate chapter on these events is that they're so incredibly boring and dreary you run considerable mental risk in attending them. Many a teacher has come unglued after listening to the assistant principal mumble his way through an hour's worth of unadulterated bullshit and the same thing could happen to you.

To avoid such a fate, here are some tips for getting through the experience without suffering a mental breakdown and going the way of so many of your colleagues.

First, arrive early in the library meeting room and get a seat that's hidden behind a file cabinet or miscellaneous furniture. If you're out of sight you can fall asleep with impunity and never hear a word said. What's more, nobody will call on you and demand that you rise before the assembly and answer some inane question. Just be sure to sign the attendance sheet or they'll never know you were even there.

If all the hidden seats are taken when you arrive and you have to sit in full view of everybody, take notes—or pretend to. Get a sheet of paper in front of you, prop your head up on one hand and grip a pencil in the other and go to sleep. With practice, you can sleep like a baby and give the appearance that you're recording the crap word for word.

*Survival Rule:* **To help survive boring teacher meetings wear dark glasses so they won't notice when you slip into a coma.**

The chief drawback here is that you may be called on and you'll be dead asleep and unable to answer. That means there'll be that awkward moment while everybody turns to look at you and watch you sleep. When you are poked awake there's the panic of knowing you've been asked a question and you have no idea what it is. A large roomful of people staring at you makes the experience all the more memorable.

In any case, deny you were asleep. Insist that you were just resting your eyes. Rub them vigorously. Blink several times. Squint. Ask them to repeat the question since you had your eyes closed and didn't hear it. Such a scenario would be embarrassing but worth it if you got to sleep through most meetings without incident.

Another danger of sleeping at meetings lies in the chance the meeting will end and everybody will go and leave you fast asleep behind that filing cabinet. That actually happened to Marv Nussbaum one day and the custodian had to wake him up when he swept the place out hours later.

Vodka is another dodge that works. You get one of those water bottles everybody carries around these days and fill the thing with vodka and tonic and sip away. By the time the meeting winds down you'll be in fine spirits and sorry to see the party break up.

Or you can bribe a kid to call in a bomb threat five minutes into the meeting and send everybody out into the parking lot where you can slip into your car and go home. Or a fire alarm might do. Or sneak in early and spray the library with virulent pepper spray so they'll have to send everyone home.

You can also feign illness just before the meeting but they're likely to get suspicious if you pull this before each and every one. Or you can have someone page you with an emergency phone call and just don't go back. Or...but you get the idea. If you can manage to evade even four or five meetings a year you'll save that much wear and tear on your nerves and be better for it.

To illustrate what you're up against, here's how a typical teachers' meeting would go at Mackenzie, or almost any other school in present-day America.

The meeting begins when the principal reads the first item on the agenda aloud and then spends ten minutes explaining what he just read one syllable at a time. Next, he calls for Ms. Klein's report on storeroom supplies and she rambles on for another ten minutes. Snores rise from distant points. People fidget. Even the principal looks at his watch and does a double take and shakes it in disbelief.

Another agenda item is analyzed in depth and Ed Collins from science is asked to report on the upcoming science fair. Ed proceeds to read an eight-page statement on the history of science fairs and their place in the 21st century. The ennui is palpable.

Some of the girls in the back who have been sharing water bottles for the last forty minutes are giggling and creating a minor scene. The principal frowns and takes a long pull at his own water bottle. More snores are heard.

Another committee report, this one from the truancy people. Fortunately, theirs is a short one as four of the five members are absent and the fifth one just returned from a six-week absence himself and has no idea what's happening with their report. But, alas, Coach Bixby uses the truancy committee's time to pitch an appeal for more lenient grades for his nearly illiterate varsity players so they can win the championship and bring honors to Mackenzie High School.

More reports follow, each drier than the last. Spirits fall right and left. People faint dead away from sheer boredom. Yawning is endemic. The principal can't stand any more and he pleads a prior commitment and skips out. Mutterings are heard, drumming fingernails, impatiently tapping feet. Finally, seconds before the place explodes and a general stampede ensues, the meeting ends and teachers flee with an alacrity that one seldom finds in people their age and shape.

And there you have it. The principal files his report and gets a check after his name, the superintendent is satisfied that all is well. The teachers go home pissed at having wasted more time on irrelevant crap and American public school education continues apace. Nothing has been accomplished; the whole business could have been handled by passing out a one-page copy of the agenda to be read at everyone's leisure.

Those who have read this excellent manual and learned the necessary survival skills will escape with the least harm to their psyches and be that much more capable of surviving altogether and making it to retirement. It's not much but it's better than nothing.

*The educated differ from the uneducated
as much as the living from the dead.*
– Aristotle

## Chapter Ten

### PARENTS' NIGHT

I read recently where somebody spent several million dollars to study attendance at the so-called parent-teacher nights where parents come to school to meet their kids' teachers and compare notes. This guy learned that attendance is high in elementary schools, not so high in middle schools, and almost nonexistent in high schools.

Isn't that astonishing? Why didn't the sap just ask some teachers and save all that money and time? The man uncovered facts known by everybody including the kids and spent a fortune in the process. Isn't that typical?

I taught at all three levels myself and could have given this bird a diagram suitable for framing if he'd just stopped by and asked me. When I was in elementary school they had to hire moonlighting cops to handle the parking. Parents came in waves. Every teacher had forty people lined up outside her door to inquire after their precious darlings. It was a memorable scene.

In the middle school there was a noticeable drop off in numbers. Parking was readily available and lines were short. Parents wore a frazzled look and chewed their lips and frowned a good deal. The kids had eyes like saucers and seemed torn between making a break for it and trying to brazen it out. So I moved on to high school and ended up at the Big Mack. I remember my first parents' night. I was ten minutes late and apprehensive lest all the parking spots were taken. I needn't have worried. The entire student lot was empty except for six or seven cars clustered at the gate.

Inside, nothing moved. The halls rang hollowly as I headed for my room. I passed Marv's room and looked in. "Where the hell is everybody?" I said.

Marv looked around. "What? Somebody's missing?"

"The parents. There aren't any. The halls are empty, no cars in the parking lot. This is parents' night, isn't it?"

"The parents are here. I saw one a few minutes ago."

"One? One parent? I thought they came in twos."

"Not around here, they don't. Nobody shows up for parents' night. You'll be lucky if you get six or seven all night. What's the point? By the time they get to high school the parents give up. The kid's either a lout or he's not. End of story."

"But why do it, then?" I said. "If you turn in your attendance and they see only six or seven people came in doesn't Central Office realize it's a waste of everybody's time?"

"But Central Office never sees those numbers. You think the principal's nuts? He multiplies the count by ten and sends that downtown. Downtown knows he's lying but they don't give a damn. The numbers are filed away and everybody's okay; we look like we're doing a helluva job and nobody's the wiser."

*Survival Rule:* **Screw-up kids and pissed-off parents are a volatile combination; stay alert and ready for anything.**

I saw six people. Two of them came by to give me a good thrashing for failing their kids and another one demanded to see my credentials but the fourth one was reasonable and sane and we had a long talk with his reasonable and sane daughter. Two others came in but they were in the wrong room.

Still, no matter how many parents show up you've got to know the ropes when confronting their larcenous offspring in their presence. These are desperate people, remember, guys with nothing to lose. Once the old man finds out the kid's been absent for three weeks running or on suspension since October or is failing every class it's curtains, anyway. This means he'll lie, file wild charges against you, whimper and whine, incriminate the innocent, even resort to violence.

Don't forget, he's desperate. I had one kid dead to rights one night and he knew it. As he entered with his hulking old man I detected a look in his eye that sent shivers down my spine. I'd no sooner opened my record book to expose his abysmal ignorance and long list of criminal acts when the sneaky scoundrel reached over, grabbed my record book, and leapt gazelle-like over some chairs and raced from the room.

But he was dealing with a pro and didn't know it. I instantly whipped another copy of the book from my coat pocket and nailed his ass on the spot. His old man was livid and left in a huff and I snapped my record book shut with a satisfied smirk.

That's how it works when you know the rules.

Watch out for the really desperate kid who brings in a ringer and tries to pass him off as his old man. The kid knows he's a goner if his parents find out what a loser he is so he gambles everything and hires some old bum to play dad. This can work since you've never met his parents but it's easy to spot the deception if you know what to look for.

One guy brought in a girl about twenty and claimed she was his mother. A white kid with blond hair and alabaster skin showed up with a black guy and swore he was his real dad. A girl came in with a ninety-year-old woman and said she was her mom. Incredible.

Guard the fire alarm boxes because kids have been known to pull a false alarm and empty the building just before their parents reached math class. Some fall down with pretend seizures. Others pray for God to earthquake the place to the ground while some try to bribe their teachers or call in bomb threats.

So watch them. There is true danger in these conferences. No one knows how far a kid will go to keep his villainy under raps and you're in the line of fire. And don't rely on this kid's parents to protect you, as they're likely to be just as loony as the kid and will end up helping him box your ears for you.

In fact, now that I think of it, parents' night might be a good day to use one of your sick days and skip the whole thing.

> *Education is what survives when
> what has been learnt has been forgotten.*
> – B. F. Skinner

## Chapter Eleven

### HOW TO USE SICK DAYS

All school systems provide sick days for teachers and the wise teacher uses them up pretty much as he goes along on the grounds that a sick day used is better than one in the bank. Many a careless teacher has saved hundreds of days and then died and left the city with a hundred grand worth of unused sick time. Don't make that mistake.

Sick days are intended to cover actual health problems like broken legs or heads or high fevers or surgery, all things most people don't experience. Though not actually sick you're sure to need regular mental health days to help you cope with the pressures of teaching in the 21st century.

But be cagey about it and keep them off balance in the manner of guerrilla fighters the world over. It's a good idea to stagger your sick days so that a pattern doesn't develop. If you regularly take Fridays or Mondays off some snoop downtown may conclude you're abusing your sick time and sic inspectors on your ass. This could lead to stakeouts on your house and other inconveniencies and nobody wants that, do they?

Also, have a care that you don't take a Caribbean cruise in mid-January and come back with a deep tan you didn't have a week earlier. You can always claim you used your new sun lamp but it doesn't look good and inevitably arouses suspicion.

Use your acting skills when calling in sick. Say you're in a blue funk. It's December and Christmas is approaching and you haven't a friend to your name. Call in sick. Get on the phone and act like a sick person. Wheeze a lot. Speak in a weakened voice, almost a whisper. Gasp for breath. It might go something like this.

"Hello, this is Jan Cramer. (Gasp, choke) I'm sorry I won't be in today. I have a code. (Wheeze) I'm on antibiotics. (Hack, cough) I think it's the flu. (Rattle, wheeze) 'Bye."

A tip. Don't overact. One guy was so convincing on the phone the principal was alarmed and sent the paramedics by to see if he was dying. Of course, he was already headed for the golf course and wasn't home when they arrived. Things got a little sticky because he overplayed his hand.

*Survival Rule:* **Sick days are yours in lieu of money; use them whenever you feel like it.**

Don't do stupid things when you're on a sick day. A guy took sick days to attend a golf outing and he won first prize and got his picture in the paper. He also almost lost his job.

What's that? Using sick time when you aren't sick is immoral or fraudulent or worse? Nonsense. It's a benefit you've earned in lieu of more salary. It's yours. They owe it to you. Everybody uses sick time without being sick. We even had a principal who took several of his staff members to Acapulco for a holiday and every one of them used sick days to cover his absence.

I know about this because they had the misfortune to run

into the guy who was in charge of school security down there and he turned their asses in. None of them was fired but all were disciplined and made to look like idiots among their peers.

As you see, administrators aren't innocents, either, though they seldom use sick time for free days off. The reason they don't is because they just claim they're doing school business and take off. They go shopping or fishing or take three-hour lunches or go to the movies and nobody ever dares ask them to prove they were really at meetings somewhere.

So take those mental health days. You can be just as sick in the heart or head as you can in the gastrointestinal tract and require time to rest and get well. Duck out to the track and breathe some fresh air. Hit the malls. Rendezvous with a lover and a bottle of good wine. Enjoy a day away from the turmoil of teaching and come back refreshed and revitalized and ready for another go at them.

After all, isn't that what sick days are for?

*Education makes us what we are.*
– C. A. Helvétius

## Chapter Twelve

### A FAILED STRATEGY FOR RECAPTURING THE SCHOOL JOHNS

Teachers find themselves engaged in an endless struggle to stay on top of things and not lose any more turf than they've already handed over to the kids. Very often these battles involve actual real estate that's occupied by unfriendly forces that have seized possession and defy attempts by the staff to regain it.

Certain areas on campus are traditionally the provinces of the kids, places like the area around the flagpole out front and the basketball courts out back and the weedy patch behind the driver ed. range among others. The geography varies from school to school but one special spot of contention in just about every school is the school john.

In most high schools the kids have long since taken over complete control of the johns. The teachers may run the building and make the rules but everybody knows the johns are inviolable sanctuaries for the students and no affair of ours.

Certainly, that's the case at Mackenzie. Teachers seldom if ever venture into the johns for fear of what they might find there. Weird noises emanate from these places, muffled screams and angry shouts and low, moaning sounds float out through the air vents and into the halls and nearby classrooms. Live band music is frequently heard. Most eerie of all, though, are the long moments of utter silence, interludes that fire the imagination and bring chills to your spine.

They apparently also hold spectator events in there as well because we'd often see kids selling tickets outside the door and long lines waiting to get in. We were curious, naturally, but not so curious as to actually go in and see what's going on.

Anyway, somebody broke into the business department's storeroom and made off with a lot of tape recorders and computers and other stuff and Tommy Slatz was really pissed about it. In fact, he was so mad he resolved to catch the crooks no matter what.

He knew the stuff would be sold in the johns so he came in early and crept into one of the johns, hung an out-of-order sign on a stall door, and hid inside to spy on the crooks. A few minutes later the first kids arrived and began setting up for the day. One kid put on a pot of coffee and another laid out boxes of donuts. Others set up tables and displayed their baggies of grass and cold beer and a three-piece combo tuned-up in a corner.

In no time the place was filled with kids and clouds of marijuana smoke as everybody lit up and the day's business was underway. Tommy crouched in the stall and took notes furiously.

Kid One: "I'll give you ten bucks for that coat, man."
Kid Two: "Hey, you're pissin' on my shoe!"
Kid Three: "You standin' in the urinal, man!"
Kid Four: "Where'd you get these donuts? These things is

stale, man."

Meanwhile, the smoke seeped into Tommy's stall and then into his lungs and the poor sap was quickly overcome and stoned out of his mind. Since nobody knew he was going into the john, we never thought to look for him there and he wasn't found until after school when the custodian opened the stall door and Tommy rolled out in a heap.

It was too late, of course. The dreaded marijuana smoke had saturated his brain and turned him into a hopeless addict. From that day on we couldn't keep the guy out of the johns and his career was cut short as a result.

Now I was pissed and determined to avenge poor Tommy, and the way to do that would be to regain control of the johns and drive the losers out for good. Accordingly, I put together a first-rate plan that would enable me to do just that, a plan that would call for lots of raw courage, nerves of steel, and the taking of extraordinary risks but I never wavered for a moment. What the hell, I teach in America's public schools; danger is my business.

Needing a crew to put my plan into effect, I dropped by the teachers' lounge to recruit volunteers from the guerrilla pool that hangs out there. I reached the door to the lounge and Leo Corelli was on his way out. I stopped to talk to him for a moment while standing at the open door and I overheard the teachers talking in the lounge.

"It's awful quiet out there," Agnes O'Rourke said, looking around as she spoke.

"Yeah, almost too quiet," Ida said.

"Sometimes you can almost hear the drums in the distance," Agnes said.

"Of course you can hear drums," Marv said. "The band

practices right above us."

"I mean different drums," Agnes said ominously.

"Everybody hears different drums in this place," Marv said. "None of us would be here if he heard a regular drummer."

*Survival Rule:* **Never enter a students' john for any reason. And never let a student in your john, either.**

"How do you know the drums we hear aren't the regular drums?" Ida asked.

"You mean it's normal for people to end up like this?" Marv said, startled.

"You guys better knock it off," old man Scanlon said from his Lazy Boy Lounger Easy Chair. "You start hearin' imaginary drums and they'll throw a net over your ass."

About this time Jan Cramer from English passed me on her way into the lounge and I finished with Leo and followed her in. Jan poured a cup of coffee and sat down with her skirt riding high on her thigh and Marv fixed his gaze thereon and watched it steadily the whole time.

"We were just saying how quiet it is out there," Ida said.

"Maybe too quiet," Agnes added, nodding knowingly.

"We just had another hall sweep," I said, pouring some coffee and taking a moment to help Marv watch Jan's thigh. "We sealed off the back hall and caught hundreds of them. We stored them in the auditorium."

"What a nightmare!" Jan said. "Five-hundred hooky players thrown together in a dimly lit auditorium."

"It makes the Black Hole of Calcutta look like a Sunday school outing," Marv said, shuddering.

"And that's exactly why I came in here," I said. "We've got to get a grip on ourselves and regain control of Mackenzie High before it's too late."

"Somebody tell him," Agnes said.

"It's not too late," I said. "We just need a plan, that's all, and I've got one. All I need is a few good men to make it work."

Ida rose and started for the door. "Good," she said. "For once sexism works in our favor. If you're looking for a few good men you won't be needing me."

"Don't move, Ida," I said. "I was using men in the all-inclusive sense, as man in mankind."

Ida sat back down. "Harrumph!" she harrumphed. "I thought I had a loophole there."

"What is it this time, Evan?" Marv demanded. "Another hare-brained scheme to make the kids go to class?"

"Well," I said smugly, "I can't tell you what it is. It's a secret."

"Gee, a secret plan," Agnes said.

"I'm keeping it a secret so the kids won't find out what we're up to." I leaned in conspiratorially. "I want all of you to rendezvous with me in the basement near the coal chute. Eight-thirty sharp Thursday. Make sure you're not followed."

I whirled on my heel and started out. When I stepped out into the hall I ran into Leo on his way back in and stopped to talk to him for a second and overheard the comments from the lounge again.

"He's wasting his time," Marv said. "The kids will have his secret plan all figured out long before Thursday."

"It was probably their plan to start with," Jan said.

At this point the bell rang and everybody made ready to get on to his next class.

"Who can worry about Thursday?" Agnes demanded. "I'm worried about surviving the rest of the day."

"Yeah," Scanlon said, heading for the door, "you work here for a while and you learn to take things as they come."

**Survival Rule: Try to assume a philosophical outlook, one that makes powerlessness appear desirable. Something from the Stoics might do the trick.**

The teachers passed me as they filed out of the lounge and left Marv there alone. I heard him sigh audibly. "Or as things take you," he said to the empty room, and marched wearily past me on his way out.

I ignored them, of course. There are always malcontents who fail to appreciate all we do for them.

So at precisely eight-thirty on Thursday my crew slipped down the basement stairs and huddled together in the plenum chamber to hear the details of my latest attempt to wrest control of the school from the hooligans who were presently running the place.

The home ec department provided us with brownies and coffee and I took the trouble to inspect them, as there'd been instances where mysterious substances had got into brownies served at teacher meetings and I wasn't taking any chances. I held one up to the light and examined it carefully.

"What are you looking for?" Marv asked apprehensively.

"Twigs and leaves," I said. "But I don't see any."

I took a bite and chewed and the others followed suit and in no time we'd polished off two or three apiece and were all well on our way to being stoned with Mackenzie's infamous brownies.

"You said you had a plan?" Ida said.

Jan had carelessly allowed her skirt to slide alarmingly on her thigh and I fixed my gaze firmly on the spot in case it should go any higher when Ida jolted me back to reality.

"Oh, right," I said, tearing my eyes from Jan's thighs and addressing the business at hand. "You all know we're in deep shit around here and it's getting deeper by the minute. I don't have to tell you how important it is that we take control back from the kids."

"How important is it?" Agnes said.

"Pay attention, will ya?" Ida snapped. "He just said he didn't have to tell you how important it is."

"How important what is?" Marv said. "We still don't know what we're doing in the basement."

"It's a raid!" I shouted suddenly.

"What?!" Marv exclaimed.

"Where?!" Jan said.

Agnes and Ida sprang to their feet and looked sharply in every direction at once and I quickly hastened to reassure them before they panicked and did something dumb.

"No, no, nobody's raiding us!" I said. "We're the ones who are going to do the raiding for a change. I'm organizing a raid on a boys' john. We'll catch the thugs in the act and arrest every one of them for drug possession, hooky playing, and throwing wet toilet paper up on the ceiling."

"We're going to raid one of the boys' johns?" Jan asked dubiously.

"Sure. It's all set for tomorrow. Ten sharp. We'll swoop down on them before they know what's going on." I held up a ditto. "It's all here on these dittos, the whole plan. Familiarize yourselves with the details and be ready at 10:02."

Agnes had a brownie in each hand and she chewed determinedly.

"What if these dittos fall into the kids' hands?" Ida said. "Won't they know our plan?"

"No problem," I said. "They won't be able to read it. I wrote it in standard English."

"Good thinking," Jan nodded.

"Maybe we should synchronize our watches," Marv said.

"Are there any more brownies?" Ida asked.

"They are good, aren't they?" Marv said. "And this is the best damn coffee I ever drank."

Agnes inspected a brownie with cocked head and said, "I wonder what they put in these things?"

My gaze had attached itself once more to Jan's thighs and I lost myself for a moment in some marvelously erotic thoughts until I was able to regroup.

"Good," I said at last. "Are there any more questions?"

"About what?" Ida asked absently.

"Good. We all know what to do then."

Marv had folded his ditto into a paper airplane and he sailed the thing gracefully through the air and straight into my forehead.

"How long is this meeting gonna last, for God's sake?" Agnes demanded. "We've been down here for hours now."

"Right," I said, frowning and trying to remember what we were talking about. "All we have to do is sum up here and we'll be on our way."

"Right!" Marv agreed.

"Okay, then. It's all set."
"Should we synchronize our watches?" Jan said.
"Good idea," I said. "I've got eight-fifty-six."
"My watch says nine-oh-four," Jan said.
"Nine sharp," Agnes said.
Ida shook her watch vigorously and stared at it from time to time. "My watch has stopped!" she said.
"You're looking at the back of it, Ida," Marv said.
"That's close enough," I said. "Meeting adjourned."
They rose and headed for the stairs and proceeded up same while I lingered behind. Jan was still in her seat, her skirt exposing vast stretches of tantalizing thigh. She looked at me with a thin smile playing about her mouth and I moved toward her driven by a mind clouded with Mackenzie High brownies.

Ah, well.

At the appointed hour the next day the john raiding party composed of Marv, Jan, Ida, and Agnes with me in the lead crept along the hallway to a spot just around the corner from one of the boys' johns. Once arrived at this vantage point we huddled together to whisper last minute instructtions and admonitions.

"You gonna reconnoiter first, Evan?" Marv asked.

"Yeah," I said, leaning out to peek around the corner. "I'll sneak up on 'em and see which way the wind blows before moving in."

"You're going right in the john after them?" Jan said alarmed.

"Have to. That's where the pricks hang out. There must be hundreds of 'em in there."

Marv nodded. "He's right. It's madness but there's no

other way."

"Well," I said grimly, "I'm going in. If I'm not out in fifteen minutes, come in after me."

They all nodded and shook their fists and made appropriate comments.

"We're right behind you!"

"You can count on us!"

I stepped resolutely around the corner and started for the john door. Pausing a moment to look up and down the hall, I squared my shoulders and opened the door. A great cloud of smoke streamed out and forced me back.

"Holy shit," I said aloud, "it looks like the place is on fire! They must be smoking dope by the bale in there!"

I took a big breath, stepped through the door, and found myself in a surreal scene full of swirling smoke and dimly seen moving shadows and rock music. When my eyes adjusted to the light I saw the place was also full of kids and all of them were smoking dope. What's even worse, some of them were smoking tobacco.

"Well," I said, "I see everybody's here—and I do mean everybody." I let my gaze sweep the room. "I didn't know these johns were so big!"

Kid One appeared from the surrounding smoke and said, "Yeah, we did some remodelin'. Knocked out some walls, rerouted all them pipes, you know, fixed 'er up."

"We made this our clubhouse, man," another volunteered.

"This is a club?" I asked dubiously.

"Yeah. A private club."

"A private club, you say? Hmm. After getting a look at you guys, I'd like to see some of the people you kept out." I surveyed the crowd disdainfully and they stared back without expression. "But I didn't come here to join any club," I went on briskly. "There's so much smoke pouring out of here I thought the place was on fire. Don't you guys know we have rules against smoking in school?"

"We has?"

"No shit?"

"Man, they never tell us nothin'!"

"And that's not all—somebody in here is smoking marijuana! I can smell the stuff right now." I inhaled a big cloud of smoke and coughed. "Anybody smoking dope in here, I'm gonna have to take 'em in. Come on, now, who's got the dope?"

Kid One handed a joint the size of a six-dollar cigar to another guy and said, "Man, you're gettin' more marijuana 'n you want every time you take a breath."

"Yeah, we oughta be chargin' you for all the free dope you're gettin' in here," another added.

"Oh, yeah?" I said defiantly. "Listen, I'm immune to that stuff. I could inhale marijuana by the pound and never bat an eye. Why, I once stood on the windward side of a burning marijuana field and inhaled the smoke for a whole afternoon and it never fazed me a bit. Why..." I was warming to the subject when I spotted a kid with a slight smile on his mug. "What are you grinning at?" I demanded angrily. "Haven't you ever seen an old marijuana fighter before?"

"I ain't grinnin'," he said.

"We don' allow no grinnin' in here," Kid Two said.

The tokers were all grinning by this time but I was having some trouble marshaling my thoughts so I accepted his reassurance rather than deal with the heavy concentration I knew would be required to figure it out.

"Well, that's better," I said, mollified. "Nobody grins at The Kid, by God."

"You The Kid?" a guy on my right said.

"That's right," I said to the guy on my left, "and don't you ever forget it."

"You're all right, Dr. Keliher," Kid One said. "It ain't every teacher will come in here an' have a smoke with us."

"Yeah," I said, suddenly woozy. I was stoned through and through and didn't know it. "Well, it's a good thing you aren't smoking marijuana or I'd have to run you all in."

"Hey, man, this is our clubhouse," Kid Two said. "We don' allow no dope in here."

"That's right," another guy said. "Jus' as quick as we see anybody brought dope in here we take it away from them an' burn it."

"Jus' like we're doin' now," Kid One said, holding up a burning joint.

"Right!" I said. "I knew I could count on you guys." I leaned closer. "And, remember, everybody's looking for you."

**Survival Rule: Whiskey will counter the effects of marijuana smoke, but you must have drunk it before inhaling.**

"Shit!" Kid One said. "No wonder we in such awful trouble all the time. Everybody is always lookin' for us."

A pretty girl walked by and I did a double take at such a sight in the boys' john. I straightened up and turned to leave. "And remember, no dope. If I catch anybody smoking dope in here, I'll close this place down and drive you all into orphanages."

I coolly surveyed the room and its occupants, then turned and walked with dignity straight into a wall. I backed off and studied it for a moment before turning to address the throng.

"All right, who put that wall there? Are you trying to make me look foolish?"

"Man, people who walk into walls don't need no help lookin' foolish," Kid Two said.

I mustered all the dignity I could command and said, "Oh, yeah?"

I headed for the door again and this time succeeded in making it out into the hall accompanied by a cloud of marijuana smoke. I adjusted my lapels, looked both left and right, and started down the hall with a heavy starboard list as I went.

I'd forgotten all about the rest of the raiding party hiding around the corner waiting for my return. They weren't paying attention and failed to see me emerge from the john and decamp.

"How long's it been?" Ida asked.

"Thirty minutes," Jan said, looking at her watch.

"Didn't he say we should come in after him if he wasn't out in fifteen minutes?"

"No, it was fifty minutes," Marv said.

"Fifty minutes!" Agnes exclaimed. "It'll be lunchtime by then. That means we'll be working on our lunch hour and that's against the union contract."

"Agnes is right," Marv said firmly. "We'll come straight back here after lunch."

They started off in a bunch, each assuring the others of his intention to go back right after lunch and rescue me. It's a good thing I was able to keep my wits about me and save myself or I might still be in that smoke-filled john even now.

The moral? Some things are inviolable, even sacrosanct. I say let them have the johns. Fight them in the halls and stairwells, stand firm in the classrooms, never say die in the lunchroom, but surrender the johns as a concession to student power and the fact that we'll never succeed in driving them out, anyway.

Remarkable.

*Education makes a people easy to lead,
but difficult to drive;
easy to govern but impossible to enslave.*
– Lord Brougham

## Chapter Thirteen

### THE COUNSELOR: FRIEND OR FOE?

And what about the counselors? What is their job, exactly? Can you count on them to help you in your ongoing fight for sanity and safety? Are they there to help you or are they on the kids' side? Remember, they're not strictly teachers themselves, as they don't have to face classrooms stuffed with recalcitrant kids whose sole aim in life is to torment their teachers and drive them nuts or worse.

The plain truth is these guys are more properly considered miniadministrators who tend to regard their counselees as delicate, misunderstood innocents being picked on by their teachers and charged with baseless crimes and misdemeanors. Many of them are failed teachers who were eased out of the classroom because they couldn't cope and kicked upstairs, a route not uncommonly followed by many administrators. They're usually gullible and easily deceived. Don't count on them.

Still, it's not all their fault, either. School counselors are a unique bunch in many ways, being curious mixtures of advanced cynicism, masochism, and borderline madness. Instead of classrooms, they live in little cubicles at the Big Mack surrounded on three sides by glass and exposed to the world like goldfish in aquariums, forever peering out and never knowing they're the ones who are locked in.

Their time is spent arranging paroles, fingerprinting students new to Mackenzie, investigating truancy cases, listening to one heart-rending story after another from kids trying to con them out of bus tickets, finding beds in homes for unwed mothers, identifying bodies, and so on. Small wonder that counselors have a higher than average incidence of mental malfunction, nervous exhaustion, and outright insanity.

Over the years, I've been privileged to watch many of them at work in their glass wombs as they struggled to help some confused inmate of our institution to a better understanding of himself. For example, not long ago I dropped in to see Marty Weiss on some minor matter and overheard the following bit of dialogue between him and one of his counselees.

"Tony, put that chair down!" Marty said as I entered. He threw his arms above his head in the classic warding-off-a-blow position and retreated to what he hoped was a neutral corner.

Even with me as a witness to his gross insubordination, Tony refused to do as ordered. "I'll put this chair down on your baldhead, you...!" he declared.

*Survival Rule:* **Don't send too many kids to counselors for discipline; they'll spread rumors that you're weak and can't control your class.**

I slipped up behind him and knocked him down with a well-placed karate blow to his carotid artery and the poor devil never knew what hit him.

"Now, Marty," I said, unconsciously propping a foot on the prostrate chair-wielder, "maybe you can tell me what's going on around here?"

"Good work," a relieved Marty said. "You saved the day, Evan. I thought I was a goner there for a minute."

"Nonsense," I said. "You'd have had him yourself in another minute or so. Why was he trying to drape that chair over your head?"

"How do I know?" Marty demanded. "The guy was mad at me because his locker had just been ripped off for the third time this semester. When I told him the official school policy denied all responsibility and that he'd have to pay for his lost books he snatched up some furniture and tried to kill me."

"Well," I said, motioning to a couple of attendants standing by, "we can't have this kind of thing going on at Mackenzie. Take him below and have him flogged."

Actually, this last scene didn't play exactly as it's written above; this is the way I'd like to see it played in my own private Walter Mitty kind of world, but what really happened was when I saw Tony raise the chair and start after Marty I rushed part way into the study hall and shouted, "Hey, you!" When the chair wielder looked around I scooted for the door and left Marty to do the best he could under the circumstances while I moved briskly along the hall calling loudly for security.

*Survival Rule:* **Always keep an eye open for a chance to change careers — and don't be too particular, either.**

Fortunately, Marty's injuries were minor ones (the

surgery went smoothly) and the entire matter ended up before the principal who held a conference with the student's mother and all concerned parties and everybody learned a good lesson from the meeting, too.

Tony learned he could do whatever he wanted to do and they'd blame his mother; the counselor learned the principal was gutless and wouldn't make waves over anything short of an actual homicide; the mother learned neither the principal nor the counselor knew what he was doing; and the principal learned he'd taken up the wrong profession and wished he'd become a plumber like his brother.

Counselors get to be counselors in various ways, not all of them entirely rational. Some become counselors when their nerves finally give out after years of teaching in the classroom, moving directly from a convalescent center into the counseling cubicle. Others are made counselors as punishment for some real or imagined crime perpetrated against the rules of the school board. And, of course, a lot of them are masochists undergoing a form of aversion therapy.

Once selected, counselors undergo highly specialized training before being sent into battle. They need a wide variety of experiences and background in order to deal with modern high school students one-on-one.

For instance, counselors are trained to detect beer on the breath of a teenager clear across a standard-sized playing field. They also become proficient at running urine tests for marijuana—a job which requires much of their time in many schools today—and can frequently be seen hurrying through the halls with racks of yellow-hued test tubes in hand.

They must learn to talk would-be jumpers (usually other counselors) down from high ledges, become handwriting experts to spot all the forged absence excuses that stream across their desks all day, familiarize themselves with all of the students' inalienable constitutional rights so they'll know which ones of them to violate, learn to overpower crazed students driven mad by the system, and generally come to grips with the day-to-day operations of the modern American high school and the people who frequent such places.

It's strongly recommended that nascent counselors have real hands-on experiences with mentally deranged individuals since they will doubtless have considerable contact with such people once they hit a real high school and have to contend with the teachers they find there. Many counselor-trainees have even cleverly disguised themselves as patients and spent months or years in various sanitariums and psycho wards to get first-hand knowledge of the techniques used in such work. (Some think they weren't phony patients at all but that's another story.)

Counselors must also be wary of substance abuse—not the kids', I mean their own. The job is so nerve-wracking and riddled with anxiety and tension that the average counselor is almost always on something before long. A lot of them are on the bottle. Some of them smoke the pot they take from the kids and end up getting hooked on the stuff and have to go into prostitution and crime in order to support their habits. Others are on Valium and speed and uppers and downers and assorted mind-altering drugs and potions required to get them through a day of meeting American teenagers face to face in a never-ending battle of wits the kids always seem to win.

*Survival Rule:* **Use emotion, not reason, when dealing with counselors; no reasonable person would have that job.**

No wonder they get stoned.

Their cubicles are usually built with walls that don't go all the way to the ceiling. They do that to be sure nobody has any privacy so every word you say can be heard by people in nearby cubicles. And, since many counselors are old and hard of hearing, their counselees have to shout the most intimate things at the top of their voices so the whole damn school will know about that parole violation or pregnancy as soon as it happens.

I saw an example of this when I stopped by the counseling center to put up some wanted posters and witnessed the following scenario. A troubled teenager entered and headed for her counselor's cubicle.

"Well, what do you want?" Mrs. Blight snapped.

The girl sat nervously and looked around apprehensively. "Uh, Mrs. Blight, I wanted to see you about..."

"What? Speak up! What are you whispering for? Speak up!"

"Well," the girl said a bit louder, "it's personal and..."

"Are you going to speak up or not?" Mrs. Blight shouted in a booming voice. "I haven't got all day, you know. Spit it out, for God's sake!"

Well, the girl was finally pissed and she shouted, "Okay, you old bat! I've missed my last three periods! There. Is that loud enough for you?"

The girl stormed out and the counselor shrugged and hollered out for the next guy in line.

Some kids try to avoid a similar experience by writing it

all down on a sheet of paper so she can read it to herself, but that doesn't work because counselors are carefully trained to recognize this ploy and deal with it.

Mrs. Blight took the proffered note from the student and glared at it.

"What's this?!" she boomed out. "A note? Hmmm. You say you missed your period?" The girl winced. "What? You missed three periods!" The girl reddened and tried to hide. "Say, Cindy Jones, just what the hell have you been up to, anyway? Do your folks know about this? I'll have to make a full report to the student council; you'll probably be expelled when this gets out..."

One more victory for high school counselors over teenage malfeasance.

Another aspect of their job has to do with helping kids choose the right courses. They analyze the records of arriving freshmen and work up a profile to determine which courses they're most suited for and then program them into something as far from that as possible.

By careful questioning she'll learn that the kid can't stand manual labor and hates to gets his hands dirty and dislikes all things mechanical and then the wily old codger will sign his ass up for a four-year course in auto mechanics and machine shop.

Counselors also offer advice on career choices but most kids don't put too much stock in this advice since it's apparent they didn't do all that well in choosing careers for themselves.

I watched a kid enter seeking career counseling and he ran afoul of the infamous Mrs. Blight.

"So, you want to be a lawyer, eh?" she said with a sneer.

"Well, I thought I..." the kid started to say.

"Are you kidding?" she snapped. "With your record you'll be needing a good lawyer before you can ever become one yourself!" She riffled through her files. "You aren't on suspension, are you?"

"No, I..."

"Look," she said, "why don't you forget this lawyer stuff and just sign up for another year of auto mechanics? They always need good mechanics, you know."

"But I..."

"Just sign right here under auto mechanics. That's right. See? Wasn't that easy?" She leaned out to call around him and shouted, "Next!"

The guy was on his way back to the auto shop and the dedicated counselor had successfully saved still another student from taking up a life of crime and rapine. Now that's what high school counseling is all about.

But enough. You get the picture. Forewarned is forearmed.

Review this chapter occasionally to remind yourself of the nature and composition of counselors and what to expect and why. They have to be handled with kid gloves to allow for their instabilities. If you can learn to deal with their idiosyncrasies, which is to say with their personas in toto, you'll find them a lively and interesting bunch.

Or maybe not.

*The direction in which education starts a man will determine his future life.*
— Plato

## Chapter Fourteen

### CATCHING CHEATERS

The kids never tire of bamboozling their teachers and making them look like saps. It's almost a tradition. The teacher brings ruin and devastation to their lives by flunking them, sending damning notes home to their parents, reporting their hooky playing, springing surprise tests, humiliating them in front of their friends by asking them questions and exposing their ignorance and a lot more.

Naturally, after all this the kids love a chance to get even by beating the teachers at their own game and one way to do this is by cheating on a test and getting a passing score without actually studying.

Your job, then, is to guard against successful cheating because every time it happens you're the object of their scorn and the butt of their jokes. They've flummoxed you again and they gleefully report it to their friends and everybody has a good laugh at your expense.

Cheating is anathema to all teachers, of course, because it's morally wrong and a sure-fire ticket to hell or purgatory or worse, but let's take a closer look at the subject just to be sure we all know where we're coming from.

People oppose cheating on the grounds that it's dishonest but this is a weak argument. Everybody cheats they just cheat on different things. We all pay the traditional lip service to honesty and strongly recommend it—for others. We teach kids that honesty is a highly desirable commodity in this world when nothing could be further from the truth.

Take another gander at George Washington and the cherry tree bullshit. Here we have a patent lie routinely fed to little kids everywhere as a fact. It's an apocryphal story from beginning to end and everybody knows it. George never cut down any cherry tree with his little ax, and if he did he tried to cast suspicion on a nearby colony of beavers just as you or any sane person would in a similar situation. This base canard only serves to further reinforce my point: hypocritical blackguards that we are, we lie even when we're trying to encourage honesty in our kids.

The fact is most people have very little regard for honesty except when it benefits them. We all want to be honest ourselves as long as it isn't too inconvenient for our own interests. It almost seems to be nature's way.

How many of us are thoroughly honest when we're trying to unload a used-car on some poor unsuspecting sap? Or when we call in sick because we want to go shopping? Or when we report on our taxes to the government? We all lie and cheat in these cases and thousands more and still we demand honesty from kids.

So? Does that mean we should look the other way when monitoring tests? Of course not. Everybody knows we work from the principle of do as we say and not as we do. How will our kids succeed in the world if we don't give good, solid examples of hypocrisy to instruct them in worldly affairs?

Besides, remember our fragile egos. Do we want to be

regarded as fools and bumblers, mocked by children, scorned? Hell, no. Keep a weather eye peeled and nail these birds and show them who's in charge, I say. And to help you do that I've outlined some common ways kids cheat so you know what they're up to and catch them in the act.

We can start with the Teachers' Workroom Caper. This is a very popular practice, one that works every time. All a kid has to do is wait until all the teachers have left the place (about three minutes after the dismissal bell in most cases) and sneak into their workroom and go through the wastebaskets, files, desks and whatnot for copies of tests, quizzes, answer sheets, etc. Our apprentice burglar then not only uses it to pass his own test but he sells copies to his crooked friends and they all ace your test.

Solution: Leave some phony test and answer sheets around so the thief can get hoist on his own petard.

Then there's the ever-popular crib note. All that's necessary here is that the kids hunt up some answers to questions they're fairly sure will be on the test and jot them down on their cuffs or on some scraps of paper or the back of the guy's shirt in front of them and copy like hell. Some kids even put them up on the ceiling so they can allay suspicion while gazing heavenward as though for inspiration.

*Survival Rule:* **Refuse to tolerate cheaters—except, of course, when circumstances require you to be the cheater.**

The girls often jot notes down on their thighs and just

slide their skirts ever higher on their legs as they need fresh answers. The main drawback to this dodge is that male teachers' eyes are naturally drawn to skirts moving up on pretty legs and the cheater stands a good chance of getting caught. Besides, if the skirts go high enough they'll paralyze the minds of all the guys for four rows in every direction and they'll flunk and their girlfriends will beat the crap out of the sliders for being shameless hussies.

That still leaves the old-fashioned notes written on assorted body parts. I've seen cheat sheets on knuckles, palms, knee caps, elbows, feet, cleavage, and bare midriffs on warm days. To catch these guys you have to scrutinize every part of their anatomy with great care. Remember to be discreet, though, or somebody will hang a sex harassment suit on your ass for ogling.

A word of caution to counselors. Another almost foolproof plan that was uncovered at Mackenzie was known as the Counselor's Aide Ruse, a scheme wherein a kid volunteers to act as an aide to his own counselor and thereby gains access to his own records. All he has to do is change all undesirable grades to more desirable ones on his transcript and stick them back in the files. Nobody will be the wiser and he'll probably win a scholarship to the Graduate School of Business at Harvard or Stanford.

Then there's the reliable 'Steal the Grade Book' plan. This one is brilliant because of its simplicity. The kid steals the grade book and throws the damn thing away. Without that record you're forced to give everybody at least a passing grade, i.e., a "C" and that includes the thug who stole your book.

Counter this ploy by keeping all test papers in a file at

home. If they steal the grade book, you can reconstruct it from the exam papers. Better still, have a second copy—or even a third—on hand and you'll come out the winner in this little game.

A lot of kids rely on simple copying from a neighbor, one of the oldest cheating tricks in the world. All one does is sneak looks at other people's answers and write them down. All that's required is steel nerves and a few basic rules on how this works.

Watch kids sitting next to Asian students with calculators hanging from their belts, as these are the people who know what's going on and the ones most likely to be copied. Contrarily, watch bikers and jocks and reefer salesmen, as they're the ones who'll be doing the copying. Look for shifty sidelong glances, hands shielding eyes, craning necks, and kids who spend a lot of time watching you so they can sneak a peek when you look away.

Also be extra alert at any distraction such as a dropped book or someone raising his hand to ask a question or any interruption like a messenger at the door, etc. Practiced cheats seize these moments to scope out their neighbor's work and good ones can copy down a page of answers while you answer the door.

Keep an eye peeled for creative guys who come up with new wrinkles. For example, I knew one kid who sat near a window on the ground floor. When he got his exam he balled it up and threw it out of the window and into the hands of his fellow conspirators who were waiting outside with a textbook and notes. They filled in the answers and threw the balled up paper back inside. Unfortunately for him, it landed at my feet and I caught the cheaters red-handed, as it were.

Well, I was so impressed with the sheer brilliance of the scheme that I let the kid take the exam over and he failed it all by himself and went on to meat cutting school where he belonged in the first place.

Be on the alert for kids using mnemonic devices. They code the answers and jot down abbreviations, numbers, symbols as prompts and even leave them right out in the open as they're meaningless by themselves and can't incriminate. Kids who are bilingual will also use notes written in arcane languages known only to them and you won't know what they're doing.

Keep an eye peeled for smart kids posing as somebody else and taking the exam in his place. In this regard, be wary of strange kids who show up for exams unannounced. A sure sign that something is amiss would be a kid named Toshio Muriyama claiming to be Paddy O'Flanigan or somebody named Mary signing in for Pete. If you don't recognize one or more of the testees, demand picture ID and proof he's a bona fide student who belongs there.

After all of the above, though, one area stands out as the one where most cheating occurs and that's homework. Nobody likes homework much and who can blame him? Kids get their first dose of the stuff in the first grade and they keep getting it for the rest of their lives. Teachers are obliged to assign homework by executive fiat and the kids resent it and continually look for ways to get out of doing it.

Some time-honored dodges employed to evade homework and make you look like a boob in the process are presented here for your edification. Familiarize yourself with their particulars and you'll be ready for them when the next clown tries one on you.

Chief among the ploys is plain, old-fashioned lying. The kid just swears he handed his homework in and you lost it. If he's good enough he'll succeed most of the time. Here's an example of one such occasion at Mackenzie when one of the devious con artists worked it on veteran teacher Agnes O'Rourke.

Juan: (feigns astonishment) "What you mean you ain't got my homework?"

Agnes: (correcting grammar) "I don't have your homework, Juan."

Juan: "But I turned it in, Miss O'Rourke!" (points) "I put it right there on your desk! I go, "Here go my homework, Miss O'Rourke."

Agnes: "Juan, I do not remember getting any homework from you."

At this point Juan goes nuts. He runs up and points to the exact spot on the desk where he put the homework, appeals to other kids for support, smites himself on the forehead, and generally acts like an innocent man wrongly accused.

Juan: "But I turned it in! You was talkin' to a girl wearin' a Knicks jacket!" (to nearby kid) "Billy, you seen me when I turned my homework in, ain't you?"

Billy: "Damn right. You put it right there." (points)

Agnes: (uncertainly) "Are you sure, Juan? I didn't see it with the other papers..."

Well, you're a goner now. That slight glimmer of uncertainty in your voice; you're not sure. If Juan refuses to give in and makes his story good enough you'll begin to doubt the whole damn thing and think maybe he's telling the truth and you really did lose it.

*Survival Rule:* **No, the dog didn't eat his homework; give the little fraud his F.**

In true guerrilla fashion, Juan now shifts gears and aims for even greater spoils. He boldly demands an A on his alleged homework because this was absolutely the best work he ever did and it was even typed and everything. In the end Juan gets credit for an assignment he didn't do and all the kids have a good laugh at your expense.

Another scheme involves excuses for not having homework when it's due. As in the absence excuse ruse, these cases have to do with cleverly conceived but entirely phony excuses used to confuse things and avoid that F.

Again, a fertile imagination is the key. Instead of just claiming the dog ate his homework the clever kid will embellish the story by presenting torn, illegible sheets of notepaper full of teeth marks and drool. The drool is a good bit because he knows you won't want to examine the sodden paper and expose him for fear of getting rabies. I've even known kids to bring a dog along as further evidence that they actually had a dog.

Another good excuse you'll get in places like Detroit is the claim that some thug held him up at gunpoint and made off with his homework. Most teachers know our cities are full of ignoramuses who regularly commit armed robbery to get a pair of sneakers off some poor sap's feet so they'll usually buy this story several times a semester. You know he's lying but what can you do?

Girls have some unique excuses they can use which are

theirs by virtue of their sex. So many teenagers are having babies these days that they can always say they don't have their homework because they had to stay up all night taking care of the twins.

One girl at Mackenzie told her teacher she didn't have her homework because she was up all night having a baby and it worked, but another girl lost her case when she told the teacher she didn't have hers because she was up all night making a baby. The teacher gave her an F even though it appeared she'd already had that.

Keep good records. Collect homework and file it away in a safe as soon as you get it. Be on your toes, pay attention. You're dealing with unprincipled people who take delight in deception and roguery and you'll be undone if you give them the slightest chance to do you harm.

The point is if you're going to give homework make sure the stuff is done and properly recorded. It's your job to see that the sharpers don't get off scot-free as the rest of the kids diligently slave away for the same grades the frauds get. You work to insure fair play even as you fight for the honor and integrity of the profession. So watch them.

One more. Run term papers through a computer and look for the original work from which the deceiver lifted it. It's easy and quick and will expose a plagiarizer in a trice with evidence that will stand up in court.

So keep on top of these guys and refuse to let them bamboozle you. If you're tough enough kids will come to know you can't be conned and will actually study to pass your tests and that's the whole idea, isn't it?

*A little learning indeed may be a dangerous thing, but the want of learning is a calamity to any people.*
– Frederick Douglass

## Chapter Fifteen

### GUNS AND HOW TO LIVE WITH THEM

Kids used to stick out their tongues at teachers when their backs were turned or even give them the finger, but nowadays they're just as likely to come up with a gun and shoot them dead. Every teacher is aware that kids can be armed and the mere awareness of such a condition turns every campus into a place of fear and danger. You ignore the notion of armed students at your own peril.

These are your true guerrillas, guys armed with real guns shooting real bullets and terrorizing entire communities. They shoot from ambush, from dry gulches and passing cars, and make no effort to distinguish intended targets from innocent passers-by. One such guy can lay a cloud of fear over an entire campus and reduce everyone's efficiency in the process.

Our first experience with gunplay happened one winter's day when the initial shock of strident student militancy first swept the country. It seems a couple of guys had a misunderstanding of some kind and one of them sauntered into the building looking for his antagonist in order to set things straight. And, just to make sure there was no further misunderstanding in the matter, he brought along his trusty snub-nosed .32 caliber automatic.

According to witnesses, the two met in the crowded halls when classes were changing and proceeded to set things straight in the following manner.

First guy: "I been lookin' for you, punk."

Second guy: "Who you callin' a punk?"

The first guy had already finished talking, though, and he came out with his gun and commenced spraying the nearby terrain with bullets.

Now, the most interesting kinds of things happen when guns make their appearance on the scene. You can't imagine the effect they produce unless you've been on the business end of a piece of machinery that can blow your worthless carcass to smithereens in less time than it takes me to write it down.

*Survival Rule:* **Always remember, the one with the gun is in charge.**

There are no heroes, everyone reacts in exactly the same way; he shows an irrepressible desire to vacate the premises just as fast as his terror-driven legs can carry him. And he doesn't stand on ceremony, either. Like the proverbial Chinese fire drill, it's every man for himself and women and children better keep the hell out of the way.

Anyway, I didn't hear the shots because I was in the teachers' lounge resting my eyes (some said I was sleeping but that's a base canard) and the transaction took place at the opposite end of the building. I first realized there was something amiss when the thundering feet of the panic-stricken mob rumbled past the door of the lounge. I'll never forget that sound. I've heard it many times since and it always announces the presence of your friendly neighborhood gunslinger practicing his trade in the immediate vicinity. The door of the lounge burst open and dozens of scared kids poured into the room in a torrent of frantic humanity. Old man Scanlon sprang from his Lazy Boy Lounger Easy Chair where he'd been zonked out for the last forty-five minutes and demanded to know what all these students were doing coming into the teachers' lounge without knocking. In the confusion I made out the words guns and shots and I ducked out into the hall to see what they were talking about.

This was a serious mistake on my part, one only a rank beginner in the arts of violence and mayhem would make. Old-timers who've ducked flying lead before have learned the consequences of such rash acts.

The hall was a disaster. I was sucked into the mainstream of a swirling river of heads, knees, boobs, and elbows and swept along the floor of the hallway as a pebble is washed along the bed of a swiftly moving stream. Nobody had any idea where he was going or even if he was going where he wanted to go, he only knew instinctively that the situation called for very rapid movement and it didn't make much difference what route he took. In a word, speed was of the essence, not destination.

*Survival Rule:* **When you hear gunfire, run. Forget about direction or destination. Just run like hell and don't look back.**

Long after the gunman had left the premises we were still careering back and forth in that hall, 800 bodies locked in a mad embrace, dancing a crazy dance of hysteria and everybody high out of his mind on the trip. We'd be there still if Sam Browne from vocational hadn't recovered his wits and started slapping faces to bring everybody back to his senses.

That was my big lesson, my survival lesson on how to make it in the new madness that had gripped our schools. I never again rushed blindly into a dangerous situation, never answered danger's call until I'd made damn sure there wasn't any danger left in the area.

And the rest of the staff learned it, too. Ever after any sound of crashing glass, blood-curdling screams, gunshots, high-pitched wailing, explosions, thundering feet, or similar signs of danger were answered the same way by all hands: we instantly found some bit of work that was so crucial it had to be done that very second no matter what. After two or three minutes we'd begin casting oblique glances at each other until a conversation running something like this would take place.

"What was that?"
"What?"
"That noise."
"You mean that sound of crashing glass?"
"Yeah."
A shrug. "I don't know. Somebody broke a bottle, maybe."
"You think that was it?"
"Who knows?"
"Think we should go take a look?'
"Maybe we should."
Now that they've waited long enough for any and all

dangerous types to clear the area, they figure it's safe to go investigate. Just as they're getting up to go, though, a long shriek pierces the air and it comes from the same direction as the sound of breaking glass. Everybody immediately goes back to step one and becomes engrossed in his work.

*Survival Rule:* **When fleeing in panic from an advancing gunman try to assume the look of someone who's just remembered an appointment he's late for and is hurrying to get there. It makes for a better image.**

We fought back where we could, of course, but ineffectually at best. Some teachers even began carrying guns themselves for self-defense. It always struck me as weird to see a little old lady from the English department practicing her fast draw in the teachers' lounge with a mammoth .44 caliber Colt her great grandfather had used to fight Indians before the turn of the century.

Bobby Carmichael wanted to strap dynamite sticks to his chest so when shot he'd blow up and take his assassin with him, but we managed to dissuade him when we pointed out he'd take the rest of us, as well.

Incidentally, before we wrap up our gun section we need to take a brief look at holdup protocol. There are so many thugs loitering around most public schools these days that you are almost certain to encounter one or more of them over time. If you're unfamiliar with accepted holdup etiquette, you may well pay with your life or more.

Suppose you're heading up the street for lunch and three or four ugly guys—these guys are always ugly—pull to the curb and call you over under the pretense of asking directions or some similar ruse. The idea is when you approach their car they'll stick a gun in your face and demand all your worldly goods.

If this should happen to you fall back on your guerrilla tactics and surprise the jokers. Feign innocence and take a step toward them to allay suspicion and then turn and run like hell in the opposite direction so they'll have to turn their car around to chase you. Nine out of ten times they'll just drive off and look for another victim who's less fleet of foot.

The tenth time, though, they'll leap out and open fire on your fleeing ass and maybe put a bullet through an arm or leg and drop you in your tracks. In that case you'll probably lose all your worldly goods.

*Survival Rule:* **Stay away from windows lest someone outside shoots you or someone inside pushes you out.**

On the other hand, if the robbers get the drop on you at close range you should throw your hands up in the classic pose of the robbee everywhere and commence begging and pleading for your life even as you struggle to remove your wallet and hand it over.

In fact, cooperation is the watchword here. Give the guy anything he wants. Address him as sir. Tell him where he can find friends of yours who carry large amounts of cash. Suggest possible escape routes for his use after he's finished robbing you. Offer to hold his gun for him while he packs your stuff in a box.

Also avoid looking these guys in the eye. If they get the idea you can identify them they'll drill you to get rid of witnesses. Whatever you do don't say, "You'll never get away with this! I know who you guys are! I never forget a face. I'll help the police artist draw a perfect likeness of your ugly mug and it'll be on the evening news!"

No, it won't. What will appear on the evening news are pictures of your sheet-clad body being loaded into the morgue wagon while onlookers search the ground for any loose change you may have dropped.

In short, don't give the guy any reason to shoot you. Remember, you're dealing with a real ignoramus here with an IQ on a par with the average chipmunk and you'll be lucky if the half-wit doesn't shoot you just to see if his gun is in working order.

Another tactic to guard against robbers is to always have your own gun in your pocket and when they pull up to ask for directions you can whip it out and spray them with bullets. You'll usually take them by surprise and will be able to plug two or three of them before they know what's going on. If you're a good enough shot you'll incapacitate the whole lot and you can rob them and teach them a valuable lesson while you're at it.

*Survival Rule:* **Learn the protocol for stick-up victims so you'll know the proper role of the robbee.**

Always remember to have some cash ready, too. There's nothing worse than a disappointed stickup guy who's just learned you're carrying a total of four dollars and a bus ticket. He'll look more kindly on you if you can hand over a thick wad of bills and a diamond-studded watch. Just consider it an investment in your health.

Discretion is always the better part of valor, to quote the

Bard, and you know what a smart guy he was. So be discreet.

Anyway, that's where we stand today. The kids carry guns in their pockets, the teachers carry fear in their hearts, stretcher-bearers carry the wounded to the medical clinic, and our mortician carries away the statistics.

Nobody really benefits from all this but it does seem to be the American way, after all.

Learn from our mistakes—or else.

> *There is less flogging in our great schools than formerly, but then less is learned there; so what boys get at one end they lose at another.*
> – Samuel Johnson

## Chapter Sixteen

### THE PITFALLS OF SUBSTITUTE TEACHING

Suppose that some calamity occurs in your life and you're forced to seek work as a substitute teacher. While I sincerely hope no such fate befalls you, if it should there are some things you'll need to know.

First, though, have you ever thought how necessary subs are? What happens when there just aren't enough to cover all the vacancies? Trouble, that's what. At Mackenzie, we tried various schemes including one where we routed all abandoned classes to the auditorium and had some hall-duty teachers watch them. We ended up with two or three hundred kids jammed in that place all hours of the day in a scene straight from Dante's Inferno complete with smoke from burning joints, high-pitched wailing, and rasping, dry bone-like laughter dripping with evil.

We held out until one day we actually smelled brimstone and the principal had to send out for a priest to come and fumigate the place with holy water and fifty pounds of incense. The priest later said he'd driven off at least a score of devils and dozens of imps and we were relieved, all right, but not happy with his bill for five grand. It seemed a lot of money for an hour's work; I thought holy men were supposed to scorn material goods and liked sleeping on cots in unheated cells, but I guessed this padre didn't fit that stereotype, as I watched him tool away in his new Corvette.

Anyway, as you can see, the place falls apart if there aren't subs available. We need good ones, or even poor ones, and we need them every day. There's lots of work for the career-minded sub today, a general clamor for his services resonates on all sides, but it's a perilous career. You get low pay and no benefits, no seniority or job security, no chance for promotion, and unlimited abuse, scorn, and humiliation. All in all, not a very good deal, is it?

But good deal or not, how can you survive the experience if you find yourself enmeshed in the subbing underworld? You'll be subjected to one outrage after another because that's the sub's karma. For example, the sub office will assign you to a subject field you have the least training in because that's their basic policy. The conversation goes like this.

New Clerk: "It's Kaplan. English. I've got six spots and..."

Old Clerk: "No, wait, we need somebody in a welding spot or...no, here's one. Send her to King High. Physics."

New Clerk: "But she's an English teacher and we need six..."

Old Clerk: "Forget it. It's board policy. She'll have to fake it."

And so she will. All over the city English teachers fill in for math people and history types cover for biology teachers and typing teachers teach shop classes. And what do you do when asked to teach kids some esoteric subject you never even heard of before? How can you teach when you can't figure out the lesson plan with a divining rod?

Consider. The physics teacher leaves the following sub plan for you.

> Dear Sub:
> The class is studying internal motion on external planes to measure K elements and the speed of vaporons. The multimometer is in the desk drawer. Use standard settings. Be sure to allow for the effects of gravity and the electromagnetic variants.
>
> NB - Check voltage so you won't electrocute yourself. Have a good day.

Now, what the hell are you supposed to do with that? Einstein couldn't decipher such crap. You don't know gravity from gravy and you're expected to follow this plan?

Well, no, you aren't. See, the secret is nobody really expects a sub to do any real teaching. Even your lamebrain principal knows English teachers can't teach physics and he doesn't give a damn. All he wants, all the school system wants is for you to keep the kids from tearing the roof off the place and they'll be delighted with your performance and invite you back on a regular basis. In other words, they don't want trouble. If you can keep order, you're a winner. Line them up in tidy rows, keep the noise down, and everyone will think you're a real pro—and you will be.

*Survival Rule:* When subbing, arrive late. Claim that 8:00 a.m. call came in at 10:30 and you hurried as fast as you could. That's all they deserve for a minimum wage.

Another thing, where will your assignment be? If it's a big city your school will be one located farthest from your home and reachable only by four-wheel drive off-road vehicles, the kind that look like small tanks and need only khaki paint to be ready for the next desert war. When you get there all the parking spots will be gone and you'll have to park in the kids' lot. There will be kids idling nearby and they may offer to watch your car for a small fee. Pay them. When you enter the building note all exits, fire-alarm boxes, the first-aid station, cops on duty and possible escape routes so you'll be ready for the odd emergency. Check in at the main office and they'll send you to your assigned classroom.

The kids will not be glad to see you; in fact, some will even be outright hostile. You are on your own and will have to survive by your wits. Your only hope is to make them think you're tough and nobody's fool and you do that by assigning written work right off the bat. No matter what the sub plans say, have them copy out a chapter or two from their textbooks. Tell them it's a new method of teaching just invented by some guru somewhere in case anyone complains, but do it as copying is very good because it keeps them from killing each other or, even worse, killing you.

If they get all copied out and grow restless, let them play a game. Choose one that requires the entire class to be blindfolded and their hands bound behind them. Or use the talking stick ruse. Explain that only the one holding the stick can talk and then throw the damn thing out of the window.

Bring your video camera along and train it on the kids. Inform them that you're conducting an experiment for the school board on ways to improve substitute teaching. The camera will record the class's behavior for review later by a newly created expulsion squad charged with clearing out the riffraff.

A word of caution, though. The odds are that someone will steal your video camera before the days out. In truth, they'll probably have it by lunchtime if not sooner. You can try to deter that by claiming the camera is hooked to an explosive device that will blow their thieving hands off if they screw with it but there's always a clown there who'll call your bluff so be smart and chain it to your belt.

You can also use a small tape recorder in this ruse. Tell them you're recording noise levels and voice vibrations so board experts can practice telling who said what in class. Hint that the police will sit in when the tapes are monitored to listen for voices belonging to wanted crooks and that threat alone will shut up half the class. The tape recorder is better than the video camera because they can't steal it as easily but the pictures are more effective in court. Still, you can't have everything, can you?

Pretend you have a bad leg so you can carry a cane. Get a heavy one, one of those blackthorn canes from Ireland with tough knots sticking up all over it and use the thing as a club to beat off assailants. Don't count on drawing any sympathy because you have that bad leg, though, as high school students today regard handicapped subs as marauding lions do injured animals when scoping out a herd of gazelles. The only good thing about the bad-leg scam is that blackthorn club.

If you never plan to go back to this particular school again and don't care what they think, send everybody out with a hall pass. Dispatch a bunch to the library and send another group off for an early lunch. Give passes to the johns willy-nilly and locker passes to anyone who asks. If you have a ready pen you can write passes for the whole damn class and cop a free period for yourself.

Don't send them to their counselors, though, as these guys are pros too and they'll be down on your ass as soon as that second kid arrives. You'll have a roomful of pissed-off counselors wanting to know who the hell you think you are and making threatening gestures involving imaginary ropes and tree limbs. Don't piss off the counselors.

When school is over shove all that written work into a desk drawer for the teacher to sort out tomorrow and get the hell out. Don't be caught there alone, and that means five minutes after the last bell. Leave with the other teachers as there's safety in numbers and lock your doors and windows as you drive off. If you have to take the bus try to get a lift out of the area to a distant bus stop lest some hooligans recognize you and do you some harm.

And there you have it, a plethora of sound ideas to help you survive in that most dangerous of all teaching positions, the substitute teacher.

I have a special admonition for teachers: Treat subs with circumspection. Win their affection. Back them up and make them feel wanted and loved. Remember, if they get pissed and quit you'll never have a free period again.

> *A teacher affects eternity;*
> *he can never tell where his influence stops.*
> – Henry Adams

## Chapter Seventeen

### TEACHING OUTSIDE YOUR MAJOR

School boards are forever looking for new ways to cut corners and make sure they have enough money to pay for their first-class air travel and luxury hotels on the French Riviera so they're always on the lookout for new schemes to flimflam the teachers because that's where the money is.

For example, look what they do with class size. If a large school system can con teachers into accepting an extra kid in each class, the resulting savings will provide a ton of money to be squandered on those junkets. So what if the district already has a higher-class size than the poorest third world country on the planet? Who cares if kids are required to sit on the windowsills and students fear going to the john because someone will grab their seats while they're gone?

The idea is to save money, isn't it? First things first. Reduce the budget, find money for crucial things like chauffeured limos and new office furniture for central staff. Whatever works is okay; it's always been so.

Teachers are never surprised when somebody comes up with a new plan to give them the business once again so when the principal asks them to fill in for a missing teacher in another department—and teach out of their major areas— most do so reluctantly and thereby lay themselves open for trouble.

And what happens? Here's an example of such an event that occurred at the Big Mack when I had to cover a math class after the regular teacher quit just as a new semester began.

I showed up a minute late and found the kids all sitting in rows like ducks with calculators in hand and expectant looks on their faces. I advanced confidently to the front of the room, fished a textbook from my briefcase, and looked at it bemusedly. My guerrilla instincts told me to bluff them and I did.

"Hmm," I said, "geometry 4, eh? One of my favorite subjects. I once won a math prize in geometry for squaring the circle. I..." An Asian kid in the first row raised his hand and I frowned at the interruption. "What is it?"

"That's impossible, Dr. Keliher," he said with a display of confidence that indicated he probably knew what he was talking about. "Nobody has ever succeeded in squaring a circle."

Aha! A wise guy. But I'm a pro, remember, and I was ready for him. "Oh, yeah?" I said. "What's your name, buddy?" And I took out my pen and wrote the guy's name down and glared meaningfully at him and let him know I was onto him, by God.

*Survival Rule:* **Refuse to teach out of your major area; that will benefit you, the kids, their parents, and the teacher they have to hire to fill the open slot.**

That done, I turned to the class and said, "Who always gets straight A's in geometry?" Two kids raised their hands.

"Okay, here's what we're going to do. I haven't done a whole lot of geometry since I squared that circle"—I glared at the Asian kid and made ready to write his name down again if he had anything further to say on the matter— "so I may be a little rusty. You two guys come up here and sit by me and everybody open his book to page nine, chapter one. Do the first five problems. Any questions see my aides. Anybody has a question on history, see me. Now get to work."

And I sat back and turned my attention to the Racing Form where plain arithmetic is all that's required to effect major changes in one's lifestyle.

Now that's how you teach out of your major. Don't commit yourself. Don't claim skills you don't have. Tell that math class you can barely count or that French class that French is Greek to you and look for a way to finesse them. It isn't your fault that the school board is made up of nincompoops or the principal is without scruples because they allow such dishonest shenanigans to go on under their direction. Just because they have no integrity it doesn't mean you have to be bereft of that commodity yourself.

It's also a good idea to get something in writing that you're out of your major against your will as the courts are fond of written stuff when lawsuits are filed and prison sentences handed out. You want to establish that you're the victim before real victims appear and sue you for incompetence or worse, a more likely scenario than you might think as irate parents frequently sue when they learn their kids have high school diplomas and yet are illiterate.

Of course you're incompetent if you're made to teach French and you've never had a French lesson in your life.

How could it be otherwise? Protest. Inform the principal that you've never been to France. Assert that you don't like croissants or Jerry Lewis. Claim a phobia re arrogance, a condition that precludes your ever mingling with real Frenchmen. Get it on the record so the judge will see that you were put upon by nincompoops and fatheads and are not responsible for the kids' unparalleled ignorance.

In other words, cover your ass. It's every man for himself these days and the devil takes the hindmost—so don't be last.

*Sex in the hands of educators is not a pretty thing.*
– Kevin Arnold

## Chapter Eighteen

### BEWARE THE DANGERS OF SEX EDUCATION

From the visible evidence in the halls of our high schools these days a course in sex education might almost seem superfluous. You could argue that the number of obviously pregnant teen-age girls in our public schools would indicate they must already have a pretty good idea of what sex is all about. They had to have some idea of what they were doing to get that way in the first place, didn't they?

These teen-age pregnancies are a fairly recent phenomenon in this country. We all remember a time when unwed pregnancy was a social faux pas to say the least. A girl so afflicted would announce she was going to live with her grandmother in another state and try to get out of town before evidence of her transgression became apparent. She'd return only after she'd delivered and safely placed the baby for adoption and then live in fear someone might find her out.

Well, that's history, as they say. Today's teenagers are no more concerned about being pregnant sans husbands than your cat would be. They not only continue to stay in school, they stay right up to the very last minute and keep everybody in a state of alarm lest they deliver during their history class and require emergency obstetrical care from the teacher. The well-prepared teacher has to be ready to act as a midwife on a moment's notice and deliver babies as they appear.

As a trained guerrilla fighter ready for any eventuality, I always kept a supply of sheets that could be torn into strips on a moment's notice and a generous quantity of hot water on hand for the day when I'd be obliged to assist with a delivery. Actually, of course, I haven't the slightest idea what you do with the torn sheets and hot water, but I understand they're required in some way. I think you wrap the baby in the sheets and pour the hot water over the mother, or maybe it's the other way around, but the really important thing is to have the water and sheets ready when the time comes.

Not only are girls no longer afraid to be seen in maternity clothes, they seem actually to take pride in their condition and behave as expectant mothers always have. It's not uncommon to hear them asking each other when the baby's due and if they're going to breast feed and what they're going to name their baby and so on.

"When is your baby due, Sandy?"

"The doctor says June 15th but my mom says it's going to be June first."

"Listen to your mom; that doctor never had a baby."

"Hey, where'd you get that cool top, Karen?"

"I'm going to call my baby Tom because that's his father's name."

"How do you know his father's name?" (This remark, especially if said sneeringly, is socially unacceptable as it can lead to violence or worse.)

These girls will stand up in class and report on the progress of their pregnancies as if they were reciting an oral book report on an adventure of the Bobbsey Twins, and their classmates never raise an eyebrow, either. It's an everyday occurrence now and nothing to get alarmed about in today's society.

One pregnant girl discussing her condition will elicit comments from half the girls in the class as they relate details of their own pregnancies. By the time these girls reach the upper grades it seems most of them have kids of their own. In fact, I used to give impassioned speeches urging them to avoid pregnancy at all costs and keep themselves unencumbered until after they'd finished their education and had made a decent start in life. Then one day it occurred to me that the girls I was talking to all had kids already and I was wasting my breath so I stopped doing it.

Well, it's clear that pregnant teen-age girls really know next to nothing about things sexual or they'd manage to avoid ending up unwed mothers. Oh, they know the mechanics, all right. They know how it happens in a kind of general way, how getting laid leads to babies and all that, but they know nothing about the details, as it were.

So it was suggested we provide sex education classes in the high schools in an effort to alert these kids as to what they were getting into when they succumbed to the blandishments of their boyfriends and let them have some. No thought was given to the junior high schools where the girls were only twelve or thirteen because they were obviously too young for such a delicate subject even though alarming numbers of girls this age are also having babies.

Our first hurdle was to agree on what kind of program

we wanted and someone suggested one of these abstinence-based approaches like Sex Respect. When it was explained that the idea was to encourage kids to just say no everybody had a good laugh and we moved on to ideas that were reality-based and didn't require basic changes in human behavior.

*Survival Rule:* **If required to teach sex ed. stock up on euphemisms and generalities. Teaching the facts will get you fired.**

Next we had to find teachers both willing and qualified to teach the subject. It's not exactly a given that the average teacher is all that knowledgeable about this sex stuff, you know; in fact, it's safe to assume the average teacher doesn't know a whole lot more than some of the kids. This is especially true of the ones who never married or even got laid so they didn't have anything sexual they could relate to from first-hand knowledge.

And some of the teachers with extensive backgrounds in things sexual might be less than desirable since such types tend to get carried away and might do more harm than good. Leering old men, for example, may have all the answers but you don't want them leading intimate discussions in sexual matters with a lot of vulnerable teenagers. You'd end up with uncomfortable kids and lawsuits.

So the principal held still another meeting and called for volunteers.

"...we feel there's a real need for a class in sex education at Mackenzie High so our kids can be informed citizens able to make intelligent choices about sex," principal Hogan said.

"Are you kidding?" Ida said. "These kids know more about sex than I do, for God's sake."

"So what?" a voice in the rear sang out. "Everybody knows more about sex than you do."

"Oh, yeah?" Ida retorted, raising her new custom-made crutch and searching for the source of the remark. "You better watch out or I'll stick this phallic symbol straight up your bazoo, you...!"

"Why not make it a directed study?" Marv said. "Let them carry out individual research projects after school and learn on their own."

"You mean the way they do now?" Jan said.

"Marv's right," Jimmy McAvoy said, "give them credit for life experience and they'll all get passing grades without ever attending class."

"No, no, we need a regular class," Hogan said, "one with a full-time teacher trained in the latest sex education practices who can show our kids how to just say no."

"Yeah, the way they do to drugs," Jimmy said.

"Yes...I mean no," Hogan said. "Look, the superintendent says we have to start a sex education program here at Mackenzie so it's not like we have a choice in the matter. If it's necessary I'll have to assign someone but I'd rather have a volunteer." He scanned the room looking for a likely prospect. "How about you, Ms. Cramer?"

Relieved that he didn't choose any of us, we immediately supported Jan's candidacy.

"Sure, Jan's perfect!" someone called out.

"Right, Jan it is!"

"All in favor of Jan teaching the sex class say aye!"

A chorus of ayes rang out and Jan was our unanimous

choice to guide Mackenzie's misguided 'teens to a greater knowledge of sex and its concomitants. Jan scowled but gamely accepted her appointment and set about establishing the school's first sex education classes.

As a new semester was just beginning, we added five sex ed. classes to the curriculum and had 2,000 applicants for the 150 openings. Some kids thought it'd be an easy three credits because they already knew all the answers while others hoped they'd get to see porno flicks or take field trips to the Playboy mansion. All of them were looking forward to the homework assignments.

But they were to be disappointed. The board of education specified a curriculum that was artfully designed to avoid offending anybody in anyway whatsoever. In other words, we were going to avoid anything controversial—you know, stuff like sex. It seems the plan was to teach around sex without actually getting involved in the subtleties of the thing.

I ran into Jan a week into the semester and she was steamed.

"Have you seen this syllabus?" she said, shaking a four-inch thick sheaf of papers in my face. "How am I expected to teach sex education without actually mentioning sex? I can't talk about abortion. I can't say rubber. No pictures. Look!" She flipped through the pages of her syllabus and pointed. "Stick figures! No anatomical detail. I can't mention birth control. No graphic references. What the hell am I supposed to do in there?"

I shrugged. "You can always fall back on the birds and bees routine," I said.

"Not if the birds and bees are getting laid, I can't. No

direct references to the sex act. It's under Subsection B."

"Well, you'll just have to fake it, Jan. Beat around the bush, bob and weave. Make them read biology books. That'll make sex so boring they won't want anything to do with it."

"If it's so easy, wise guy, why don't you just come in and show me how it's done?" Jan said.

A trap! But my administrative training stood me in good stead as I quickly recognized it and stalled for time.

"What?" I said.

"You heard me," Jan said. She grabbed my arm and pulled me toward her classroom just as the bell sounded. "Come on."

"Wait!" I said. "I just remembered I have a meeting to...!"

"Don't give me that crap," she said. "You're on your way to the teachers' lounge to smoke a cigar and you know it."

"But...!"

It was too late. I was in the room and Jan closed the door and moved to the front.

"Class, this is Dr. Keliher and he's volunteered to teach today's lesson on... well, you know. Dr. Keliher?"

Caught, by God! Still, I figured I should be able to keep ahead of a bunch of fifteen-year-olds so I plunged right in.

"Okay, class, what's the topic for today?"

A girl raised her hand. "Where do babies come from?"

I studied them warily and went into my bobbing and weaving mode.

"From test tubes," I said. "From test tubes and Petri dishes."

"Then how come I'm pregnant?" another girl said. "I haven't been near any Petri dishes."

"Um, well, um, maybe it's... parthenogenesis," I said in a

rush. "Yes, that's probably it." I looked at Jan and she looked at me with unconcealed scorn. "What the hell, it happened before so maybe..." I trailed off lamely and the whole class looked at me with general disgust.

"It was Jason," a third girl said.

"What?" I said.

"Jason. He knocked her up. That's how Dorothy got pregnant."

"Oh, Jason did it, eh?" I said.

Dorothy nodded. "Yeah, an' it wasn't even supposed to happen 'cause we did it when I had my period an' you know you aren't supposed to get pregnant if you're havin' your period."

Her classmates nodded and concurred in this bit of folklore and a guy in the back said, "How come Jason isn't using a condom?"

"Good point," I said. "And that's exactly what this class is about. The straight facts. Birth control, basic plumbing, assigned reading in the Kama Sutra, nature's own plan with the..."

Jan loudly cleared her throat and brought me back to reality. I was not only in violation of several general admonitions against teaching anything truly meaningful about sex but I was about to breach Subsection B specifically!

I quickly regained my wits and went into my cover-your-ass mode.

"Uh, look, I think that's about enough discussion for today, don't you? Why don't you, uh, take out your biology books and read around in them for a bit, eh? And answer the questions at the end of the chapter."

"Which chapter?" Dorothy said.

"Whichever one you're reading," I said.

The kids grudgingly hauled out their nine-pound biology books and opened them to randomly selected pages and were instantly overcome with almost palpable ennui. I rolled my eyes and headed out with Jan close behind me.

"So that's how it's done?" she said in a voice dripping with sarcasm.

"So you're right, it can't be done," I said. "Stick figures just won't cut it. Change the course to health and teach them how to brush their teeth and wash their hands. Christ, Jan, what's the point? Give the saps what they want. They want you to go through the motions so just do it. It's not your responsibility."

"But if I'm not responsible," she asked wistfully, "then who is?"

Well, she had me there.

So consider yourself forewarned and refuse to teach sex ed. Claim you belong to some obscure religion that forbids discussing such things. Or tell them you find such talk stimulating and you're afraid you'll become aroused and hit on the art teacher again. Or hint that you're a charter member of Sexaholics Anonymous and fear suffering a relapse. If you don't heed my warning you'll find those screwballs from the Sex Respect crowd suing you for poisoning the minds of their children with bizarre things like the truth and it's not worth it.

*Poverty has many roots,*
*but the tap root is ignorance.*
– Lyndon B. Johnson

## Chapter Nineteen

### PAY AND PERKS

What survival plan would be complete without a word on teacher pay and what to do about the sub-standard wages they've always paid you? While teachers are likely to continue receiving less than their due, there are a few things you need to remember or they'll slash your salary to the poverty level.

For example, let's consider the ever-popular salary schedule and how it came about. Once, many years ago, some town aldermen were worriedly going over the town budget and lamenting the high cost of services they had to provide the taxpayers.

"Look here," the mayor said, frowning, "we're paying out almost ten grand in teachers' salaries and I say it's a disgrace!" (This was a long time ago and a very small town.)

"Yeah," seconded the judge, "and they're always harping about being underpaid. You'd think they'd be glad just to have a good job with a solid future."

"No question about it," opined farmer Brown. "They get paid more'n they're worth. I say we give 'em a pay cut and use the money we save to give the aldermen a raise."

"But won't they raise hell if we cut their pay again?" the town doctor said.

"Don't forget, we cut their pay three years ago and some of 'em are still gripin' about it."

"Boys, I got an idea," the mayor said with a conspiratorial glint in his good eye. "We have to out-think 'em and I know just how to do it. I say we give 'em a raise!"

Cries of disbelief rang out.

"What?!"

"A raise? Are you gone daft?"

"We're tryin' to save money, not throw the stuff away!"

"Hear me out, boys," the mayor said. "I said we should give 'em a raise but that doesn't mean they get more money. Truth is, they get less but they think it's more."

"Walt, if you can pull that off, you're a cinch for Congress in the next election," the judge said.

"It's simple," Walt went on. "Think about the average teacher. You got a woman, right? No husband 'cuz we won't let 'em be married and still teach school and she's always real young. So what happens is she teaches for two or three years and gets married and quits and we hire another new teacher to replace the old one."

"So?" Doc said.

"So, we tell 'em we're gonna cut their pay on the front end and give 'em a big raise on the back end. We'll start 'em real low and give 'em pay raises every year for ten or twenty years until they get a salary that's way higher than the one they earn now."

"And damn few of 'em ever work long enough to reach the top pay!" exclaimed the judge.

"It's brilliant!" Doc said.

"We'll call it a salary schedule, make a big thing of it," Walt said. "We'll be able to hire better teachers and actually end up paying everybody less over the long haul. We'll save a fortune here."

And so it came to pass. When nearby towns heard of the swindle they all adopted salary schedules with incredibly low starting salaries and the real money at the far end, money few teachers were ever around long enough to earn.

The plan was such a success that we've had it with us ever since. In these days there are school districts that spread their salary increases over as many as twenty-five years or more and still constantly threaten teachers with salary cuts, unpaid vacation days, layoffs.

I say enough is enough. Call in the N.E.A. brass, summon the A.F.T. honchos and tell them you want the salary schedule shortened from twenty-plus years to something more like four or five tops. Cops and others routinely reach their top level of pay in this time frame and so should teachers. Let them know you're wise to them and insist they dump the salary schedule dodge and do it fast—or else.

And what about the so-called merit pay plan? Now, there's another fraud being advocated by people who have exactly the same agenda as our hypothetical aldermen. Merit pay is nothing more than a plan designed to save money by rewarding a few at the expense of many.

Consider. The modern-day aldermen raise the maximum salary to giddy heights even as they rig it so almost nobody ever reaches the top. How? Easy. They use quotas. Few teachers get the top pay because every merit plan ever proposed contains quotas, i.e., no more than a given number can be a "master teacher" at any one time.

Suppose you make the top pay a hundred grand but you limit the top jobs to, say, 5% of the staff. So you end up paying four or five teachers the hundred grand and everybody else thirty-five because you have these quotas that limit the positions available.

*Survival Rule:* **Merit pay is a con; refuse to consider it—and get the guy who suggests it.**

And what if it happens that 70% of your teachers are truly outstanding and deserve master status? They won't get it, period. The school district saves money and the teachers take it on the chin again.

Another thing. Who decides who gets to be a master teacher? Why, the principal, who else? Imagine this scenario. Principal Snarf and assistant principal Bill Spanner meet to decide who gets the promotion to master teacher.

"Okay, let's see who's on first here," Snarf says, employing the usual sports metaphor that comes from years of coaching.

"Well, there's Carl Hooper here..." Spanner says.

"Hooper? Naw. He's a wimp. I don't like the guy." He picks up another folder. "Now Slimovitz here is more like it. I like his style."

"But Hooper has his doctorate from Harvard," Spanner goes on in a vain fight for sanity and reason. "He was named Teacher of the Year for two years running and he's been teaching for eighteen years. Slimovitz has only been teaching for two years and he's a phys ed. major from East Bayou U..."

"Listen, Slimovitz coached the junior varsity last fall, didn't he?" Snarf says. "And he helped put on the sports bust and he drove the team bus, right? I say he's our man.

Who else you got?"

Bill shrugs and says, "How about Thelma Green? She's a Ph.D. candidate in Modern Languages and won the Langdon Award for..."

"Forget it. She looks like a man. I hear she might even be a lesbian. Sure as hell looks like one. I say we go with Tom Rizzo. He plays third base on our softball team and he's one hell of a player. Besides, he dates my daughter and..."

Sound familiar? Is this better than the current practice of paying everyone the same salary? Will you gain from a scheme that pits teacher against teacher in competing for a carefully limited number of raises thrown in your midst like grain to chickens?

Of course not.

All this leaves aside other profound objections such as how you justify paying people vastly different wages for the very same job and on what basis you choose your master teachers when the classes they teach differ enormously in ability, family background, motivation, etc. If no two teachers ever teach exactly the same class, how do you differentiate between them?

Another thing. A merit plan can only apply to about half the staff because there's no way to measure academic achievement in many courses. For instance, how would they evaluate the coaching staff? Or the art teachers, shop teachers, business department, music staff, librarians, special ed. teachers, counselors, school nurse, driver ed. crew, drama department, et al?

Whenever you hear some sleazy politician urging merit pay, call him on it. Demand to know if there are quotas—there always are—and point out to him what a complete jackass he is. Vote against him and all like him and let them know you refuse to be flummoxed again.

Rally 'round and take a stand against the world's aldermen and demand an end to these fraudulent schemes and insist on pay commensurate with your real worth. You owe it to yourself and those who come after you.

And while you're at it keep an eye on the politicians and media types who decry teacher tenure and demand it be stopped. Fathead Bill Bennett loudly brayed that 25% of America's teachers—that's you he's talking about—are incompetent. These guys claim our kids are failing because we can't fire the incompetent teachers who are to blame for their failure. They talk of so-called bad schools and the bad teachers in them and how they need to be fired withal. Even California's lamebrain governor Arnold came out stridently against tenure in hopes he could abolish the law and fire the hordes of inept teachers who are hanging on to jobs they don't deserve.

*Survival Rule:* **Offer to surrender state tenure when the rest of the country agrees to give up civil service benefits—and pols give up lying.**

And isn't that the irony of ironies though? Politicians talking about incompetence in others is so laughable even the incompetent are entertained by it.

What about perks? Teachers have always enjoyed traditional perks such as free paper clips, broken pieces of chalk they can take home to their kids, lots of lined writing paper, textbooks, rubber bands, staples, and #2 pencils. Refuse to give up any of this loot. Accept it in lieu of a golden parachute, the kind the school board voted for your superintendent.

What the hell, it's the least they can do.

> *Ignorance is not bliss—it is oblivion.*
> – Philip Wylie

## Chapter Twenty

### VOUCHERS

Do you need a target for your next guerrilla outing? Then take aim at the voucherites massing out there because few things threaten American education more than this ill-conceived raid on our beleaguered public schools. Even though the threat was dampened awhile back when California voters hung still another heavy defeat on the voucher crowd, the threat is still very real today. It should be every teacher's duty to watch these guys and see that they don't do something irregular when we aren't looking.

The plain truth is, vouchers will destroy the public schools and everybody knows it. The voucherites know it, too, and they just don't care because most of them already have their kids in private schools and would be delighted to have the rest of us help them out with their tuition costs.

In other words, the voucher people are often a cut above the average in income or they wouldn't be educating their kids privately. Their own kids face little chance of being left behind by fleeing voucherites, then, and that means they don't have to be concerned with what's left behind for the ones who won't get out.

There'll be no health programs such as vision screening because they cost too much. No specialists to deal with particular problems requiring their expertise. Very little counseling, as counselors adversely affect the teacher-pupil ratio and wreak havoc with the bottom line. Everybody will have to figure out his own transportation, as there will be no school buses because they cost too much. No phys ed. programs such as varsity sports for the same reason.

In other words, for most kids vouchers would result in a much watered down program because the entrepreneurs running the schools would be cost conscious to a fault just as any businessman is and they'd tend to provide a minimum of services and keep an eye on profits. We've already seen that happen in some of the schools run by for-profit companies in cities where they've experimented with this idea.

Vouchers are important to the religious far right, those with kids already in private schools, elitists, and plutocrats generally. People who can see beyond their own pocketbooks and understand the severe consequences of such a failed system oppose vouchers.

*Survival Rule:* **Resist school vouchers and denounce their advocates for their cupidity since that's what motivates them.**

In any case, kids will not learn better then than now. This is merely another in a very long string of so-called reforms all of which have failed completely in the past and will continue to fail in the future. Test scores will not improve just because some kids are moved across town and into a storefront school with a CPA as principal. Oh, the top kids will always do well no matter what system you put in place because those kids are the most able and will learn almost in spite of what we do to them. The majority will fare no better than they currently do, though, and most will actually be even less successful than they are now.

Finally, there is the undeniable fact that vouchers do not raise test scores. The GAO released a study in 2002 on the efficacy of vouchers that included 78 voucher programs in 38 states involving 46,000 students and $60 million in tuition and showed that the voucher kids had no better test scores than their peers in the public schools. The literature is replete with similar studies.

I might add that the much ballyhooed charter schools are just another version of the voucher fraud perpetrated by like-minded lunatics. Countless studies have exposed their inadequacies. Los Angeles is in the process of licensing dozens of charter schools as I write and this is handwriting on the wall we cannot afford to ignore.

The same can be said for the for-profit outfits like Edison; they've run schools in several cities and struck out every time. Of course, that's predictable when they have to make a profit and can only do so by cutting expenses such as salaries, benefits, smaller class size, and so on.

What does all this mean to teachers? It means you'd better pay attention, that's what it means. Sign up volunteers. Organize hit squads. Raise enormous sums and take out full-page ads denouncing the voucherites as scoundrels. Hold huge rallies. Find out who's against us and launch smear campaigns to impugn their honor and motives. Go after the home schoolers. Insist home schooling parents have at least a middle school education and an IQ no lower than 80.

And remember to support our own candidates, the people who'll vote the vouchers down even more emphatically than the huge majority California rang up last time. Offer to serve as poll workers and steal pro-voucher votes. Challenge suspicious looking voters and demand they prove they're citizens before letting them vote. Help ferry the ballots to the counting center and throw away those from pro-voucher districts. Claim you're an official poll-watcher and you have to look over their shoulder while they vote to make sure everything's on the up and up and intimidate them by clearing your throat or coughing if they start to check the wrong box.

The thing is, vouchers are dangerous and so are the people who favor them. These guys will sell us out if they can and we've got to stop them by hook or by crook. Talk it up among your colleagues. Brainwash the kids. Threaten to flunk the ones whose parents are pro-voucher if you can do so without being obvious. Expose vouchers for what they really are and save both your career and your country in one fell swoop.

So, keep an eye on the lunatic fringe crowd. If these fatheads ever have their way you'll be working for minimum wage in a storefront school that would be deemed third-rate in Afghanistan. Your career, such as it is, hangs in the balance.

> *You can get help from teachers,*
> *but you are going to have to learn a lot by yourself, sitting alone in a room.*
> – Theodore Geisel

## Chapter Twenty One

### THE CHAINING OF THE DOORS

Walter Feldspar, a man rumored to be a real rock when it came to standing fast in the face of heavy odds, was the first principal at Mackenzie High to chain the doors in an effort to keep the thugs and hoodlums out of the building and the bona fide students in. The move was illegal, though necessary, because it violated the fire laws demanding that all outside doors be kept open in case of fire. It became a matter of chains or chaos and Feldspar opted for chains.

Years ago, when schools were normal and occupied by regular kids, the halls would be totally lifeless during class time and would only fill with students when the classes changed at the end of each period. In these times, though, there are mob scenes in the halls at all hours of the day that are reminiscent of Hollywood extravaganzas employing casts of thousands.

Every idler and thug not actively in prison somewhere saunters into Mackenzie High and wanders the halls peddling dope, brandishing firearms, setting fires, and generally giving everyone a royal pain in the ass. The hall wanderers represent one of the major problems in Mackenzie and everyone would really like to see something done about them.

Anyway, just at Thanksgiving the incumbent principal broke under the strain and had to be taken away in one of those canvas coats with the wraparound sleeves. He ranted and raved and declared he'd never be taken alive even as they were loading him into the wagon. He'd only been at the school a month and had been doing fairly well until the pot smoke from the johns saturated his brain and drove him sane. Once he understood just how dangerous the place was he collapsed under the pressure. They shipped us another principal as soon as they could get one through the enemy lines and that's how we got Feldspar.

Feldspar was astonished at the condition of our halls and immediately began casting about for ways to clear them out. An investigation showed that most hall-wanderers were non-students who infiltrated the place at will and even took up permanent residence in the building. The principal decided they'd have to go.

A meeting with the department heads was called for the purpose of divining some way to keep these intruders the hell out of the building. We met one day in the teachers' lunchroom just after the place had been fumigated so the roaches were reduced in numbers to the thousands rather than the more usual millions. Still, even as we sat there, the roach hordes were engaging in frantic group sex in a mad rush to fill the ranks of the fallen.

Feldspar made a moving plea for unity urging us to work together to put an end to the menace that threatened our school. Then he called for suggestions from the floor and got the usual assortment of half-baked ideas and crazy schemes. Finally, Sam Browne, head of the voc ed. department, offered a suggestion that eventually led to an answer.

"Why don't we hire armed guards and put them on every door?" he asked. "Then they could keep the outsiders out and just let the students in."

"Yeah," Ed Collins from science said, "but we've got so many doors in this place we'd have to hire a brigade of guards to cover every door."

"Well," Jack Ryan said, "why don't we lock all the doors except one or two and make all the kids come in through the same doors? Then we could get by with only two or three armed guards."

"We can always chain the doors from the inside," Sam said.

That struck a responsive chord. It was clear that the idea of chaining the doors held some promise of success and we ran the thing through our minds to consider the various aspects of the plan.

"Isn't it illegal to chain the doors?" assistant-principal Bill Spanner said.

"Who says so?" Ed demanded belligerently.

"The fire marshal for one," Bill replied.

"Well, who's gonna tell him?" Coach Bixby demanded. "What he doesn't know won't hurt him."

"Yeah," Bill said, "but he comes around often enough that he'll find out pretty damn quick on his own."

"Suppose we chain the doors and give the keys to certain key people," Feldspar said, "and whenever the fire marshal comes along we tip our people off and the chains can be removed until he leaves."

Everybody agreed that would be a workable plan and the very next day we bought a mile of inch-and-a-quarter chain and eighty-five heavy-duty padlocks and hung chains on every outside door in Mackenzie High School except for the main entrance out front and the door leading to the parking lot. We had them by the balls now and believed we'd struck a blow for law and order and the American way of life.

In general, the chaining of the doors was an unqualified success and helped considerably in reducing the numbers of hall-stalkers prowling through the school. We were immensely pleased with ourselves and in no time at all the whole thing went to our heads. After all, we reasoned, if chaining the outside doors was so successful, why not start locking classroom doors and keep out still more intruders?

**Survival Rule: Con the principal into chaining all exterior doors. It's okay, he's the one who'll go to jail, not you.**

And so we did.

By then we were hooked on the power of chains and locks and it was decreed that custom locks be installed on all inside doors with deadbolts and chains added for extra security. Next, we locked all the lavatories because students were rendezvousing in them to plot mischief and outrage against us and, incidentally, to smoke pot, snort coke, and guzzle beer.

It finally got to the point where everybody had to carry seven pounds of keys in order to open those doors he was required to use each day. A trip through the building that used to take a few minutes now took up to an hour because of all the locks that had to be unlocked and done up again. Yet, in spite of the inconveniences caused by encountering chains and padlocks every time you wanted to leave or enter a given place, the system ran reasonably well and we gained steadily in our running duel with the thugs.

A warning system was designed to alert the hall guards whenever the fire marshal put in an appearance so they could scurry around and unbolt everything until he left the school. And we didn't have any problem as far as evacuating the building was concerned because nobody ever left the school for fire drills, anyway.

We might have gone on this way indefinitely if it hadn't been for Law Day, a pseudo-holiday by Pres. Eisenhower to counter the Communists' infamous May first celebration of their totally bankrupt economic system with parades and martial displays in Red Square. As a result, every social studies department in America is required to round up a windy old judge who hasn't been indicted for fraud lately and show him off in the auditorium on May first. The garrulous old grafter will tell a lot of sordid little lies about everyone being equal before the law and how it's best to work within the system (which has been so good to him!) to bring about change, and other such rubbish, and the department head will be off the hook for another year.

I got the Hon. Cyrus Crabbe, a vicious old tyrant famous for giving out the toughest sentences in the Midwest, as a speaker, arranged for the men's glee club to do a number, and was ready with my Law Day program.

Everything went smoothly enough for about three-quarters of the show and I thought we might even get out of the thing alive when disaster struck in the form of a tear gas attack. The kids have these cans of pepper spray or Mace or whatever the hell the stuff is and they periodically spray a wing of the building whenever they want to close the place down for an hour or so. The stuff doesn't really bother the eyes the way real tear gas does, but it attacks the throat to a point where you just can't breathe and causes you to hack and cough as though you'd just dumped a cup of hot pepper down your gullet.

Anyway, a dozen of these degenerates opened fire simultaneously and laid a cloud of that stuff all over the auditorium. Naturally, everybody commenced coughing and hacking and clawing his way to the lighted exit signs to find the doors chained shut. The only door in the place that wasn't chained was the one we'd all entered by.

Well, it was an awful sight. A thousand minds snapped as one and everybody went completely berserk. The judge himself sprang from the stage in wild flight and promptly disappeared under hundreds of churning feet. All the people on the south side of the auditorium wanted to go north while the easterners headed west in the belief that salvation lay in that direction.

It took nearly twenty minutes to get everyone through that single exit and out into the fresh air. Fortunately, no one was killed in the crush of bodies, but a lot of people were wearing welts for many days after the Great Gas Attack.

As for the judge, I know he got out even though I didn't personally see him make his escape because that same afternoon two cops showed up in the main office and hung enough arm and leg chains on Feldspar to secure Houdini for a long weekend and led the unfortunate man away. We never saw him again.

Needless to say, all chains were removed from all doors that very day and the thugs and hall-wanderers rejoiced.

The moral here? Don't stage any Law Day programs, for one thing. And never allow yourself to become personally involved in chaining doors that are supposed to be left unlocked. Don't agree to be a key holder, don't act as a lookout, don't pass any countersigns. You know the very first time you do a raging inferno will break out and hundreds of kids will be piled high and roasted nut brown at your chained door and you'll end up in the big house.

Beyond that, Feldspar's rout is further support for the thesis that your leaders don't know what they're doing, but surely you must know that by now. I just like to reinforce it now and again.

*The thing most feared by school administrators is that they may be demoted and forced to go back to the classroom.*

– Anon

## Chapter Twenty Two

### GETTING PROMOTED

After you've been teaching for a few years you'll begin to show the first signs of shell shock, a phrase coined in WWI to explain the pitiful condition of soldiers so traumatized they were turned into khaki-clad zombies. Your eyes lose their sparkle; you appear to have cataracts the size of dimes. You develop various nervous twitches, spasms, tics. Paranoia sets in and unfounded (or founded!) fears overpower your ass.

Actually, this description fits pretty well everybody at Mackenzie. Shattered nerves and advanced paranoia were commonplace. So many people were so afflicted that normal people seemed wild and unpredictable by comparison.

Anyway, this is a survival plan so how do you deal with things when you reach this stage? That's easy. The smart ones move on to new careers with less stress and angst. They become firefighters and cops, international arms runners, shark hunters, bomb experts, commuter airline pilots, deep-sea divers, lawyers.

Others turn to drugs, prescription and otherwise. Teachers at the Big Mack were forever pulling bottles from pockets and purses and tossing down pills of every color imaginable. Invariably, they'd swallow a pill, brace themselves as it went down, and shudder as it hit home. Moments later they'd don a sappy smile and nod agreeably and be okay for another hour or two.

Some drank. They kept thermos jugs filled with unknown substances close at hand and took frequent pulls from them. Some were so daring as to include olives or onions or bits of lime to add color. Most ended badly, victims of the pernicious drug alcohol and vicious abuse and humiliation at the hands of children.

Still others went completely nuts and had to be rounded up by the paramedics and hauled off to psychiatric wards where they were given 50,000 volt shock treatments, thoroughly reconditioned, and sent back to work as counselors. They weren't entirely cured, of course, but everybody knows you don't have to be entirely sane to be a counselor.

**Survival Rule: When you're burned out, exhausted, broken, move into administration and have a good rest.**

Well, as you can see, none of these options is all that desirable. Choosing among drugs, booze, and madness is to choose cures almost as bad as the illness. There is still one other choice for those without scruples, without conscience, without pride.

You can always get promoted to administration.

How does one do that? It's the same everywhere. Whether you're teaching at Mackenzie or in some farming community in the rural South or in the frozen wastes of North Dakota, the process is the same: you polish apples and don't look them in the eye—or yourself in a mirror.

Everybody thinks about getting promoted sooner or later because they see their own administrators at work and quickly realize they don't do any. Most administrators hang around their offices or stand around in the halls or scurry off to meetings and never actually do anything that could be construed as work.

This scenario develops. Ida Crocke is talking in the hall during class change with a teacher new to the trade. Assistant-principal Spanner scurries by with his usual clipboard and harried air.

New teacher: "What the hell does that guy do all day?"

Ida: "Nothing."

New teacher: "What's the clipboard for?"

Ida: "It's just a prop. It's the old army game. Carry a clipboard and a pencil and everybody thinks you're working."

New teacher: "What the hell, I can do that."

And a new applicant for the administrative ranks is born.

The first thing to do to get a promotion is to transfer over to the phys ed. department. Studies show that three-quarters of all administrators are former jocks so that's where you need to be. But you don't have to actually work as a coach; it's enough if you're identified with them.

Sign on as the coach's assistant. Hang out with the other jocks. Learn to drink lots of beer and smoke those little cigars. Swear a lot. Go to all the games and talk sports, booze, and sex. In other words, become one of the boys because these are the very guys who constitute the pool from which new administrators are pulled.

Once you're a member of the gym door crowd your promotion is assured. The superintendent will know you by your first name. Board members will invite you on their annual picnic. Your peers will begin to distance themselves from you since they still have intact integrity and will be loath to associate with people of your kind.

What if you're female and can't be one of the boys? You have to be one of the boys' girls. Learn to lead cheers. Attend their softball games and learn to squeal with delight at their athletic shenanigans. It helps if you can also pretend to like beer and cheap cigar smoke. Go to their sports busts so you can meet the superintendent on his own turf and score points as one of the boys' girls. Offer to drive the team bus and...

What's that? You find this degrading and humiliating? You wish to be promoted purely on your abilities and skills and not on how well you can kiss the behinds of a lot of stuffed shirts and good ol' boys? Then clearly you're unfit for promotion and will never rise above your current station, as there is no other way to become an administrator—and never was. You'll either haul yourself to those softball games or give up any thought of promotion.

Once promoted, life becomes much cheerier. For one thing, you never have to deal with kids anymore except in the abstract. You will be an authority on everything. While your own classroom was totally without discipline or order, you now tell others how to maintain control and deal with offenders. Where your own lesson plans were unintelligible and aimless, you now advise others on how to write proper plans.

You'll have an office and your own phone. You'll be paid several grand more than common teachers for doing far less real work and you'll never be held accountable for anything again. You'll be able to arrive late and go home early, stay home sick without tapping into your sick bank, take long lunch hours and play grab ass with the secretaries and/or boys in the shop.

So hurry on down to the gym and sign up to drive that team bus.

> *Books were my pass to personal freedom.
> I learned to read at age three and soon discovered there was a whole world to conquer that
> went beyond our farm in Mississippi.*
> – Oprah Winfrey

## Chapter Twenty Three

### ASSORTED DISCIPLINE DODGES

One of every teacher's biggest headaches is maintaining discipline and order in the classroom. In fact, a chief cause for an unsuccessful probationary period that results in being canned is that the teacher can't get the kids under control long enough to teach them anything.

The principal goes by your classroom and hears the sounds of utter chaos emanating from within and he's naturally concerned. He peeks in and sees the air filled with paper airplanes and kids dancing on their desks and throwing lighted matches at each other and writing on the walls with magic markers and smoking cigarettes and he hurries back to his office and orders supervisors out from downtown.

I've seen it happen many times. I recall one innocent young man who'd been studying for the priesthood when he decided to give teaching a try. When he showed up I saw that he knew nothing of the real world and did everything I could to set him straight.

"Tom," I said, "you've come from a world of prayer, hope, and forgiveness. You're used to dealing with honest people, reliable people, people of a higher sort who behave rationally and intelligently. Well, we don't have anybody around here like that. This is the real world. God can't save your ass at the Big Mack, Tommy. You've got to kick butt to make it here. It's you or them. Now, here's what you've got to do."

So I laid it out for him. I told him what to look for, how to out-maneuver them, all the little tricks I'd learned over decades of public school teaching that had enabled me to become a grizzled old vet within reach of that prized pension.

When I finished he looked at me with his sad cocker-spaniel eyes and said, "I appreciate your advice, Dr. Keliher, but I think I can reach these kids with kindness and understanding. They've been ill treated by society and lack spiritual direction. I'm sure if I just explain how important education is to them, they'll see I'm right and come around nicely." He started off but turned for a parting shot. "You just have to relate to them on their level, Dr. Keliher."

He sauntered off and I shook my head in silent wonder.

The guy lasted almost a whole month and then he came to me one day and said he'd heard a voice urging him to go back to the seminary at once and he was on his way even as he spoke. He lit out without a backward glance and I later learned he'd retired to a Trappist monastery and taken a vow never to speak again—or have anything to do with anyone under sixty for the rest of his life.

Would he have made it if he'd taken my advice? Of course. And what was that advice? Okay, start off on the right foot. When the kids enter on that first day, stand outside the room and do the pointer routine again. Flex the thing and slash the air with it from time to time. Frown sternly.

Most important of all, look them in the eye as they enter and don't waver. Stare them down. Practice staring fiercely into a mirror and don't blink. Eye contact alone can give you the upper hand if done properly. If a kid stares back as if to challenge you, keep your gaze locked on his and call him over. Let him know you're wise to him and will make a point of fixing his wagon good if he makes a false move.

"Hey, you," you say, stopping him in his tracks and making sure to keep him fixed on the end of that steely stare. "What's your name, pal?"

You take out a pad and make the usual great show of recording the guy's name, then follow up with a series of questions aimed at further weakening his resolve and strengthening your own.

"Who's your counselor? When were you last suspended? Are you on parole? How many times have you failed English 4?" By this time the kid's sorry he ever made eye contact and it's not likely he'll do so any time again soon.

When you finish with this guy and send him on his way spin around quickly and glare at the kids in the room. You'll see that every last one of them looks away to avoid meeting that eye of doom and you'll know you've gained the upper hand—at least for now.

Two things happen here. The kid realizes he's dealing with a tough cookie and uncertainty and fear fill his heart and make him more tractable. Even more important, the other kids see you nailing a tough guy thirty seconds after meeting him and your reputation spreads like wildfire. By lunch they'll be talking about the mean bastard teaching English in 308 and your future will be secure.

Assign seats according to the guerrilla manual. None of

this 'everybody sit where you like' crap. Write it down on a seating chart and allow no unauthorized seat changes. Assign seats by sex, size, color, and religion. Put Sikhs in the back so people won't have to try to see around their turbans. Mix colors and races randomly so you can't be charged with assorted civil rights violations, prejudices, whatever.

Mix girls and boys, too. Gang members go down front where you can keep an eye on them. Put some big kids close to the door, as it'll be hard for itinerant gunslingers to shoot around them and hit you.

*Survival Rule:* **The penultimate step—call the parents in and hope to hell they're not spare-the-rod types.**

Who sits where will determine how hard it is to keep things under control and the principal off your neck. You need to understand the ramifications of group dynamics and mob psychology if you're going to be one of the survivors and nowhere is that more true than in seat assignments.

For example, always reserve the very last row of seats for the losers. When a kid enters the room and heads for the last row of seats mark his name down in your record book and note the word "loser" next to his name. And then plant him up front where you can watch him. You'll want those back seats later for the hard-core types who pose a direct threat to everything you hold dear.

You can check it out for yourself. Who's sitting in the last row in your room right now? No-Neck Knudsen from the football squad; Bojangles Jensen, professional truant; Ernie Wamp, reefer salesman, et al. These guys sit in the back because they believe they're less likely to be called on back there. Little do they know that such a move immediately draws the teacher's attention and she zeros in on them and watches them with a jaundiced eye. If a spitball sails across the room, look quickly to the back row. The odds are one of its inhabitants launched said spitball and you may catch him in the act if you're quick enough. If somebody drops a gun on the floor, look to that back row. An explosion rocks the room? Same advice.

All kids know that teachers tend to call on kids who catch their eye and therefore they'll look every which way except straight at you. Watch for the ones who slink behind a textbook when you're peering about for a likely target or the kid who becomes engrossed in examining a hangnail or feigns a seizure. They're playing mind games with you and you've got to out-think them.

Some kids attempt to sit behind a fat kid who weighs three-or four-hundred pounds whose bulk would hide an entire Scout troop. Some slump down in their seats and try to blend in with the floor. Others sit utterly still in the knowledge that movement attracts the eye and it does. Your eye will slide right over the still ones and light on some yahoo in the back row who's flapping around in his seat saying, "Hey, look at me!"

Seating charts. Don't start class without them.

Moving along. Never ask a question of the class at large. For example, don't say, "Who knows where Rangoon is?" Such a question invites idle remarks from everybody and trouble ensues. Instead, say "Bill, where's Rangoon?" A question directed at one kid invites a single response instead of a chorus and gives you much better control.

Don't allow card games, radios, food or drink, dope

smoking, dancing, and similar entertainments to take place during class. Nothing contributes more to a breakdown in discipline than these activities. Tell them right from the start you won't tolerate such goings-on—and don't.

Keep swearing to a minimum. Naturally, the kids will swear no matter what you do but don't make an issue of it. It will be hard enough for you to curb your own foul mouth as it is without worrying about everybody else's.

Here's a typical scene in a typical classroom in one of our typical large cities, i.e., my own room at Mackenzie.

Sally: "Hey, teacher, Billy keeps grabbing my ass!"

Me: "Hey, Billy, how many times do I have to tell you to leave Sally's ass alone?"

Billy: "Man, I didn' even touch her ass."

Sally: "Are you callin' me a liar, asshole?"

Billy: "Who you callin' a asshole, bitch?"

And so on.

More tricks. Can you make a kid write, "I will not throw little Bobby out of the window again" 500 times as a punishment for doing that very thing? No. His parents will sue you and drive you from the profession and into the poorhouse. Nor can you make the jackass wear a dunce cap and sit on a stool up front where everybody can shoot spitballs at him.

And you can't smack his behind, either. We used to be allowed to use corporal punishment but the courts ruled too many teachers were getting a buzz out of all those whippings when some of them starting introducing chains and certain leather items. You also can't tweak their little noses or pick them up by their ears or give them a good hard shoulder squeeze that leaves bruises. No vicious whacks with a ruler on the knuckles or sneaky jabs from that pointer sans rubber tip, either.

Even mental discipline is verboten. No mass punishment. No sarcasm. No lectures dripping with sneering contempt, no Chinese water torture cures or subtle threats, no waterboarding, no mass hypnosis.

(All of the above are okay if you teach in a parochial school because those places are teeming with nuns and who's going to sue a band of nuns?)

If there is a single semi-reliable weapon at your disposal in this discipline business, it's mom. On the first day that you meet your new classes, let them know your intentions. Spell it out so even the hardened criminals know where you're coming from.

"Okay, listen up," you say, moving around the perimeter of the room and keeping your back to the wall. "My name's Dr. Keliher, a.k.a. Dr. Doom." Slash the air with that pointer for emphasis. "In the immortal words of Gen. Haig at the White House, I'm in control here. This is my room. I make the rules; you follow them. Any questions?"

Ignore questioners but make a mental note of their names because they'll likely cause trouble later. "If you refuse to obey my rules, I won't play games with you. No extra homework. No staying after school crap. No trips to your counselor. No minuses in citizenship. I go straight to your parents. Screw up and I'm on the phone. I can't whale the stuffings out of you but mom can and you know she will, too. So fill out these 3X5 cards. Put your name in the upper right hand corner and write your phone number down in big block numbers so I won't have to squint to see it."

All right, you've impressed them. Now you need an

example. The very first time a kid gives you any trouble, call that parent. Fill her in with the details. Present witnesses, facts, evidence. Suggest possible punishments, severe ones. Offer to hold the little tyrant while she clobbers him good. Have her come by the school for a conference and that will really piss her off. In any case, you must follow through!

In no time the kids will know it isn't smart to screw around in your class and you'll have reduced potential trouble by 90% or more. Try it. It really works.

If the parent turns out to be a screwball who sides with her psychopathic offspring and swears he's innocent and it's all your fault because you pick on poor junior, etc? Is that it, then? Are you without further recourse? Fortunately, no. A new development recently occurred in Kentucky that will brighten your outlook considerably.

It seems a Spanish-language teacher was plagued over a two-year period by a kid who was so disruptive the woman was unable to teach effectively. The guy baited her and made vague and not so vague threats against her person. She lost thirty pounds and retired two years early because of the pressure of dealing with the half-wit.

*Survival Rule:* **The ultimate step: sue them!**

When the teacher went to the administration for help, her tormenter was given 40 minutes' detention and she hired herself off to a lawyer and sued the kid for screwing around in class and causing her great mental stress in the process—and she won!

It's true. The court awarded her $33,700 and sent bright rays of hope radiating out to schools across the land as it handed teachers another powerful tool to use in their ongoing struggle against spreading chaos. This may well be a hallmark case, one that forever changes the face of school discipline and enriches untold numbers of long-suffering teachers in the bargain.

It's all about survival, remember.

## CHECK LIST

(Twenty Sure-fire Ways to Better Discipline)

**Rule 1**: <u>Start Tough and Ease Up Slowly</u>

Coming across as a warm, friendly, easy-going type is a classic mistake made even by experienced old-timers who should know better. It's all imagery and the first impression you make will be the one they remember. You want to start these new kids off with the idea that you're a tough guy, a person who will brook no nonsense. In other words, you want to instill just a smidgen of raw fear, keep them off balance. Let them know that you're in charge, know all the tricks, and will make it hot for them should they get out of line.

Should you fail to do this kids will perceive you as an easy mark and go berserk en masse. Once that happens regaining control will require extraordinary measures and may even be impossible.

Remember, start tough. You can always relax and be your real self gradually over the first weeks, but the kids will know by then they're dealing with a real pro and you'll be off to a good start.

**Rule 2**: Keeping Kids after School

Don't do it. First, keeping someone after school means you have to stay to make sure he does and you end by punishing yourself.

Second, the kid will miss his bus and you'll have to drive him home while he smirks the entire way.

And third, it's against the law. You'll be charged with kidnapping or worse and sent into durance vile for many years and be the butt of jibes and snickers ever after.

**Rule 3**: Assign Board Work

Trouble often starts in the first few minutes of class. People are still finding seats, talking, sharpening pencils; you may be detained in the hall for a moment or two and confusion results. Seeing a chance to do mischief, the kids run amuck and trash the room just as the principal arrives with the entire school board on a tour of the building.

Avoid such a scenario with board work. Have an assignment on the board when the kids enter. Make it a written assignment, a long one that can't possibly be completed in the time allotted. Kids are to enter, take out pencil and paper, and commence writing.

While it doesn't matter what they write try to make it something meaningful, as you're a pro and won't waste the kids' time with simple busywork out of a sense of professsional pride. Collect this work periodically and record credit so the kids feel the work really matters. You can even base the odd quick quiz on board work every week or so.

The point is, kids start off on the right foot and that sets the tone for the rest of the period.

**Rule 4**: <u>Assign Seats</u>

Always assign seats as the mere act of doing so underscores your authority. Let the kids sit where they like as they enter, then arbitrarily move some hither and yon. Potential troublemakers should be separated, i.e., gang members wearing the same colors should be spread out in the room and not allowed to form a bloc where they gain strength by numbers.

Always have a seating chart for each class as an up-to-date seating chart indicates you're on top of things. Seating charts should always be affixed to your lesson plans when submitting them for administrative review. Use the charts to learn kids' names and to take attendance. Be sure charts are always available for subs. Keep all old seating charts, class record books, and similar stuff to use as evidence of your professionalism should your lunatic principal try to fire you for incompetence. Incompetent teachers don't keep good records; everybody knows that.

**Rule 5**: <u>Get a Tape Recorder</u>

Kids today are crafty and cunning to a remarkable degree and will devise ever more ingenious plans to entrap you. Still, you are a university graduate and should be able to outsmart children. For example, kids will swear your version of a particular incident is a complete lie and that you're just out to get them because you had their brother last year, etc. They can be most convincing.

How to counter this dodge? Easy. Get a tape recorder, a small one that clips on your belt or slips into a handy pocket. Anytime a confrontation arises with a student, whip out the recorder and turn it on. You can even hold it up and encourage the rascal to speak clearly so the message will be nice and sharp when you play it back for the police.

It's easy and cheap and it works, as even registered toughs fear electronic equipment.

**Rule 6**: Don't Rely on Counselors

Don't send behavior problems to their counselors except in an emergency. The counselors will resent you for unloading your work on them and spread rumors that you're weak and can't control your students.

**Rule 7**: The Parents' Role

Your ace in the hole. Most kids do not want their parents involved in any way and such foreknowledge gives you an edge. Let the kids know you won't play games; one warning and it's straight to the parents. Reinforce this dictum by having the kids fill out 3x5 cards with their home phone numbers and samples of their DNA.

Follow through. The kids will test you; don't fail the test. At the first signs of trouble call the troublemaker's parents, outline the problem, and suggest another incident will require their presence at the school for a conference and possible suspension hearing.

See that the kids know of your actions. Explain how you've had to call parents to intercede on behalf of a certain troublemaker, and glare meaningfully at the culprit while you make this speech. You need to set an example and when you do the rest will know you mean business and act accordingly.

What if the parents are loonier than their troublemaking offspring and threaten you for picking on him? Why, stop by the counselor's office and score some Prozac and grin your way to sanity.

**Rule 8**: <u>Dress for the Part</u>

We live in casual society these days and that's a good thing, but it can be a snare and a trap, too. Take it from me, dressing like a professional will help the kids perceive you as someone of consequence, someone who commands respect. A sport coat for men, maybe even a tie if the weather permits, dresses or neat pants outfits for women.

Am I suggesting a dress code? No, but smart teachers will impose personal dress codes because they work.

**Rule 9**: <u>No Dunce Cap</u>

Never employ this time-honored custom these days lest you be sued by massed Dunces outraged at such a blatant attack on the civil rights of Dunces everywhere.

**Rule 10**: <u>Avoid Corporal Punishment</u>

Alas, the good old days are gone. No longer can the teacher rap a kid's knuckles with a ruler. No more subtle jabs with pointers sans rubber tips, no arm squishing, ear pulling, nose tweaking, rib gouging. No paddling, either. Corporal punishment is out unless you find time spent with lawsuits and bankruptcy courts entertaining.

**Rule 11**: <u>Homework Assignments as Punishment</u>

This can work if not overdone. You may assign additional homework as a punishment for misbehavior but make sure it's meaningful work. Just as with the board work discussed above, give assignments tied to class work so you'll look like a pro if the kid complains and you're hauled before the school board for some vague rights violation you didn't know existed.

Check the homework and record credit.

**Rule 12**: <u>Move Troublemakers</u>

Move troublemakers to new seats if they make trouble due to their present one, but don't move them more than once as the kids will see it as a sign of weakness if you continually move them about like so many chess pieces and nothing more comes of it. A second offense requires stronger action.

**Rule 13**: <u>Use Humor Sparingly</u>

Very often you can disarm troublemakers by using humor. A ready wit, a clever remark may defuse a tense situation and make people laugh who were scowling moments before. But you must have wits to be witty so be careful here.

Too much humor may cause you to be perceived as a jokester, someone who doesn't have to be taken seriously, and you'll lose credibility.

**Rule 14**: Don't Make Unenforceable Threats

Never threaten to suspend a kid for life or make him copy the entire Oxford English Dictionary as punishment. Such empty threats undermine your credibility and make you appear weak. Besides, it will be hard for the administration to support you if you're guilty of irrational actions such as the above. Instead, remain calm and think before you speak. Assign extra homework, deny him recess, call his parents, all are okay because you can actually do these things and make them stick.

**Rule 15**: Calling on Kids in Class

A reminder: never speak in this manner: "Who knows the answer to...?" Such a query may elicit responses from a dozen kids at once and add to the overall confusion.

Instead, call on specific kids as in, "Bill, tell us all you know about the Bill of Rights. Take five minutes." This way, only Bill will answer and order won't be disrupted by a chorus of voices where only one is required.

**Rule 16:** Install TV Cameras

If you have a lot of discipline problems, i.e., more than six or seven an hour, install a video camera to record sight and sound of all that happens in the room. Point it out to the kids.

Say, "Kids, that's a video camera. We're taping the whole show. Every word and act will be recorded on tape and used by the principal to expel your ass forever. No more lying. We'll play the tape for your old man and he'll whale the tar out of you. Any questions?"

Incidentally, you don't even need a working camera, just one that looks intact. The kids will never know the difference. Pick up a busted camera, nail it to the wall, and presto! You're in show business.

Your lamebrain principal won't let you install a video camera? No problem. Whip out your cell phone, start taping, and nail the rascals with incontrovertible visual and audio proof of their guilt. Don't we live in remarkable times, though?

**Rule 17:** Don't Count on the Principal

Principals don't get to be principals by taking tough stands in support of their teachers against angry parents in discipline matters. In fact, the principal will be irritated when his afternoon nap is interrupted by the arrival of No-Neck Knudson whom you've just sent down for discipline and he'll add your name to The Principal's List of troublemakers to be dealt with later.

You're on your own and will get little real help from others. And that, after all, is the reason for this work.

**Rule 18:** The Desk-in-the-Back Dodge

Move the teacher's desk from the front of the room to the back where you can watch them but they can't watch you. You can sneak up behind a troublemaker and catch him unawares or spot a cheater by watching the backs of their heads and nailing anybody who appears in profile.

Even more, this dodge works on another level, as well. When the kids enter the room on that first day and see your desk in the back, they'll know at once they're dealing with a real pro and you've got a psychological edge right at the start. It's the subtlety of the thing, the suggested nuance of control that lets them know who's in charge. It may be a small thing but it sets a tone and we've already remarked on how important imagery is these days where appearances are more important than substance.

**Rule 19:** Pay Troublemakers Off

If the situation is nearing chaos, follow the time-honored traditions of American diplomacy and pay them off as we did the Barbary Coast pirates in the early 1800s. Get the ringleaders aside and give them the odd buck to shut the hell up so you can teach.

I know one principal (later assistant superintendent) who regularly carried a pocketful of dimes he used to placate kids and buy their cooperation. He was promoted to a central office job when he ran out of dimes and the emotional stress made him unfit for frontline duty.

**Rule 20:** The Eyes-in-Back-of-Your-Head Ploy

Place the odd small mirror in out of the way spots where you can see the kids unbeknownst to them. If you can turn your back to them and still sharply reprove some miscreant without turning around word will spread that you have supernatural powers and your reputation will grow exponentially.

***************************************

And there you have it, twenty ways to maintain discipline in the classroom that actually work. No college of ed. mumbo-jumbo, no front office bobbing and weaving, but workable, hard-hitting, practical ideas that will give you the jump on them and a chance to do some real teaching for a change.

You may want to include this list with your lesson plans as a reminder.

*There is no royal road to geometry.*
– Euclid

## Chapter Twenty Four

**SCHOOL REFORM: A WASTE OF TIME**
(Don't skip this chapter. It's the most important one in the entire book.)

Do you have any idea how much time you waste every year on busy work concerned with curriculum matters and other assorted wacko plans to fix the schools? Every time you turn around someone has another cockeyed scheme with a sure-fire innovation that will turn every kid into a scholar overnight. You end up on endless committees, spend boring hours listening to gibberish, write up reports and recommendations and generally screw away whole days and even weeks to produce nothing. What a drag.

Fortunes are spent every year in school districts all across the country on so-called curriculum study committees for the avowed purpose of restructuring the kinds of things that go on in our public schools. The money spent on coffee and crullers and free lunches for committee members alone would balance the books for the most profligate of school systems—and all to no avail.

*Survival Rule:* **Everything has been tried before and none of it works. Avoid anything new.**

For example, we had to throw out the much-heralded "new math" that some half-wit foisted off on us in the 'sixties. We now know that the system resulted in a national disaster for the eighteen- or twenty-million kids stumbling around the country who can't add up their grocery bills to prove it. When we assess our real losses in terms of money, time, and the damage done to our kids we see how much better off we'd have been if we'd just let good teachers go on pounding the multiplication tables into all those thick little heads the way good teachers have always done.

Where are all the curricular innovations of the last fifty or sixty years? What happened to the idea that television was going to revolutionize education and what happened to the millions of TV sets all the schools bought in boxcar lots back in the 'fifties?

Why hasn't the widely acclaimed team-teaching approach resolved at least some of our problems if it's so effective? Where are all the educational parks, alternative schools, individually prescribed instructional programs, learning activity packages, teaching/learning units, tutorial plans, educational technology schemes, and schools-without-walls deals?

What happened to outcome-based education ploys, values education programs, peer tutoring plans, school-within-a-school dodges, whole language methodology, and dozens of other fraudulent "innovations" once regarded as major breakthroughs in education that promised to save us from ourselves? Why are our public schools still in such heavy trouble if these "reforms" that cost countless millions of dollars were any good?

In spite of all these so-called reforms to raise achievement levels one could fill volumes with examples of static test scores with little trouble, but maybe a final example will suffice to prove that reform never succeeds. More than 1.26 million high school graduates took the vaunted Scholastic Aptitude Test (SAT) recently. The scores on this test range from 200 to 1600 points evenly divided between verbal and math sections. The scores are combined and read as a paired item.

Once again, one might assume that effective school reforms would be reflected in improved SAT scores over the years, but one would be disappointed. The highest combined SAT scores occurred in 1963 when the national average rose to 980 (478 verbal and 502 math). The verbal score hasn't changed at all since 1996 while the math average has risen slightly in the last year but both are still under the 1963 numbers. The fact is that SAT scores almost never change in a significant way no matter what we do.

Incidentally, an examination of current SAT scores will show higher levels than mentioned here because the test was re-centered in 1995 when 100 points were arbitrarily added to all scores. The theory was that the old scores were thrown off because so many more people take the test these days that the numbers aren't truly reflective of the students' real accomplishments.

Nonsense. In 1951, some 81,000 people took the SAT; in 1963, nearly a million students took the test and that was the year when the highest combined scores occurred. If the added test takers had any adverse effect on scores, the 1963 scores would surely be lower rather than higher. Additional test takers have, it would appear, no adverse effect on overall scores. In other words, re-centering is actually test rigging on a national scale to imply higher scores than are earned.

The net result is that SAT scores have not matched 1963 levels in forty seven years while we've launched numerous reforms from the New Math fiasco in the Sputnik Era to Whole Language Instruction in more recent years. Again, we see no improvement that could be credited to any so-called school reform; instead, we see a constant sameness no matter what we do to raise achievement levels.

Do we never learn?

As for you, have no truck with anything new. If it wasn't around in the Middle Ages, it's a fad. Keep a wary eye on all would-be reformers and refuse to aid and abet them in any way. If the principal forces you to sign up for some harebrained scheme that wouldn't make sense to the average hare, pretend to go along but work to circumvent his schemes where you can. Point out the plan's deficiencies, claim the same plan already failed in six other cities. Hint that the superintendent may have a commercial stake in the thing and suggest the plan may be Taliban inspired.

***Survival Rule:*** **"Relevant" and "accountability" are crap alerts; you'll soon be mired in the stuff. Don't make eye contact.**

For it won't work. No matter the plan—or the earnestness of its creators—it will ultimately succeed only in wasting your time and the taxpayers' money. It will go the way of its predecessors to make room for the next harebrained scheme that is being whipped into shape at this minute by some committee somewhere.

More proof? Let me quote the late Dr. Theodore Sizer, a renowned expert in the field of school reform and a man who held top posts from Harvard to the Annenberg Challenge and beyond. When interviewed by an *LA Times* reporter in the mid-nineties Dr. Sizer was asked if he could name a single reform in the last fifteen years that had been successful.

He reflected for a moment, then replied, "I don't think there is one."

I submit that the good doctor would not come up with such an example if he went back to the Spanish-American War in search of one for there simply isn't any.

However, there is considerably more evidence to support the charge that we're beating a dead horse in our efforts at school reform. For example, we know that graduation rates never change significantly. In 2008 the graduation rate for the country was 69% and that's about where it always is, somewhere around the low seventies. If this number is more or less constant what does that tell us about the efficacy of our reform efforts? Wouldn't one reasonably expect some increase in graduation rates if our reforms actually worked?

Conversely, of course, our dropout rates also never change appreciably even though these numbers are routinely rigged by every school district everywhere. San Diego schools claim a dropout rate of 6% or so, a figure that is an outright lie promulgated by the administration so they won't look quite as bad as they are. All efforts to discourage dropouts fail; the numbers don't lie.

In short, school reform is impossible.

How do we know that? We know it because we never see

it. Just as Stephen Hawking proves time travel is impossible because of the self-evident fact that we never see any visitors from the future, so does the same logic reveal that no reform has succeeded because we never see an example of it.

Consider. If there had ever been a single "reform" that actually did what it advertised, i.e., helped kids learn better, faster, easier we'd all know about it because the word would spread like wildfire as schools and districts and states adopted this wonder in wholesale lots. We would immediately—or at least soon—see improvement everywhere and standardized test scores would rise and Japanese and German educators would flock here to see how we did it.

There is a further factor that accounts for our inability to raise everyone's achievement level to lofty heights. School reform efforts to do so are akin to plans to make everybody average, a statistical impossibility. Such reasoning fails to recognize differences in ability, that we are not all equal in spite of our claims to the contrary. In plain truth, some kids are smarter than others by virtue of genetics, by natural talents inherited from parents or a favoring environment. It follows that some will do better than others in the academic arena and even in life generally.

In other words, it also follows that a given student's failures are attributable to insufficient ability, a negative attitude, lack of self-discipline, poor study habits, and similar factors that will forever stand in the way of a society of scholars arising from any so-called reform. As in all of man's history, our schools will adhere to the irrefutable laws of nature where one-third of the students will do quite well, another third will do tolerably well, and a third will always do least well. It's time for the realists to assert themselves.

The plain, unadorned truth is we can't improve on the original model. The old ways were, and still are, the best ways. We have it officially from no less a figure than Euclid himself. When the Pharaoh said he wanted to learn geometry the sage explained that he would have to study long hours and memorize the contents of a fat math book and solve hundreds of really hard problems. The Pharaoh complained all that hard work would be infra-dig and demanded a shortcut.

Euclid famously replied, "There is no royal road to geometry."

There wasn't then and there still isn't. Reform movements fail because no one can come up with an idea that works better than the old one. Ergo: we should stop all efforts at school reform. No more New Math or Whole Language schemes leaving millions of damaged kids in their wake. No more wasted billions. No more seminars, workshops, idylls in the woods to learn the latest fad. No more lost teacher time engaged in meaningless and worthless crap.

As with Hawking's logic, it's self-evident. The concept of school reform is fatally flawed and the evidence is there in plain view for all to see.

*Why should we subsidize intellectual curiosity?*
– Ronald Reagan

## Chapter Twenty Five

### PROFESSIONAL ORGANIZATIONS

As we've seen, while this book is a manual on guerrilla warfare it is also a survival guide aimed at helping teachers live long enough to retire in one piece. That being the case, a few brief words on the role of professional teacher organizations are required because these groups are the chief source of support for all teachers in their unending struggle for an even break.

There has been much talk of late about the value of unions in these times and even encouraging reports that many people are showing renewed interest in them. That's a good sign for working stiffs—teachers—because without the American Federation of Teachers and the National Education Association teachers would be in even more trouble than they are.

*Survival Rule:* **Join and support the N.E.A. and the A.F.T. both for your own sake and for that of tomorrow's teachers.**

In pre-union days, teachers were subject to the whims of autocratic principals who could transfer "uncooperative" teachers to schools clear across town with a wave of the imperial hand. There was no appeal. To incur the wrath of a single principal could and often did result in the loss of one's career. Few teachers would care to return to those times.

Wages were lower than a snake's chest back then, too; it wasn't unusual for teachers to live at the poverty level while fully employed. Most teachers worked two jobs because they couldn't live on their salaries, a practice that still continues even to this day. I always worked part-time and every summer and was only spared this ten-year grind when my wife began teaching and brought the family income up to a livable level.

Wages have risen to a point where teachers at the top salary can almost claim to be truly middle class, tyrannical principals have been considerably reined in since the trade's Dark Ages, and we have the combined efforts of the National Education Association and the American Federation of Teachers to thank for it. Until these organizations appeared on the scene teachers were left to fend for themselves and that meant they were effectively defenseless. How does a single individual make herself heard in a confrontation with powerful figures in the administration?

People put their careers on the line in those years. Early union members were harassed, transferred around willy-nilly, even fired. They went on strike when it wasn't a popular thing to do so teachers today could enjoy some of the benefits they have now. Everyone in the profession owes a certain debt to the efforts of a lot of people who fought for their dignity and integrity and took a stand at great personal risk to make the teacher's lot a better one.

It's all about collective bargaining and a chance to

participate in the system and strength in unity and respect and fair play. If teachers are to keep the gains they've made and continue to play any role in the business of running the nation's schools and their own lives, they have to do it through their professional organizations or not at all.

So, support the N.E.A. and the A.F.T. Let them know what you think. Write them, call them, keep posted on what they're up to and be a player yourself. After all, it's your career and your future we're talking about here.

> *When a true genius appears in the world,*
> *you may know him by this sign,*
> *that the dunces are all in confederacy against him.*
> — Jonathan Swift

## Chapter Twenty Six

### THE OFFICE STAFF

All schools have a main office where the principal hangs out and it also houses secretaries, bookkeepers, clerks, et al. Much of your business will be done with people in the office and it's essential that you have some insight into these guys so you can outwit them.

All secretaries take a special course in handling teachers, a course that emphasizes a haughty attitude and thinly veiled contempt that's designed to let teachers know who really runs things in the school. No secretary is ever hired who hasn't mastered these skills, and they even have to go back for in-service refresher courses at scheduled intervals.

Chief among these types is the head secretary, a woman easily spotted as she always has her desk squarely in front of the principal's door as a kind of barrier to keep out intruders. No one enters without her permission; everyone quakes under her penetrating gaze. She is a woman of enormous power and not one you want to cross.

She gets her power by her hold over the principal. He's usually insecure and confused and she capitalizes on his weaknesses by assuming his role for herself. In the end she's in charge and he's reduced to a mere figurehead. She sets his schedule, decides who can see him, keeps track of troublemakers (teachers who cross her) and reports them to the principal so he can fix them at his leisure, writes recommendations, official reports, policy statements and assorted billets-doux and forges his signature to them without a backward glance.

In short, the head secretary makes herself invaluable to her boss to the point where he knows he can't run the place without her and she becomes the principal in everything but name.

I've seen many head secretaries in my time and I've made a study of them. I noticed they use the same tactics with teachers that we use with kids, i.e., look tough and bluff with might and main, and it starts the moment a new teacher arrives in the main office.

New teacher: "Uh, excuse me, but I'm the new science teacher and..."

Head secretary: (glares) "Can't you see I'm busy here?"

New teacher: "Well, no, I can't. I mean, you're just standing there and..."

Head secretary: (whips out note pad) "What's your name?"

New teacher: "Marcia Adams. I..."

Head secretary: "Adams, eh?" (writes) "Now, for your information, Miss Adams, I'm the head secretary here. Do you know what that means?"

New teacher: "I guess it means..."

Head secretary: "It means it's a good idea to get along, Miss Adams. Let that be a word to the wise. You go along to get along. Now, if you'll come back sometime next week, I'll see if I can get you a parking decal. You'll have to park on the street until then. Oh, there's a time limit on street parking; you'll have to move your car every two hours."

Miss Adams has crossed the head secretary and will live to regret it.

There are several ways to deal with these birds but most of them aren't legal. You can always try to win them over with kindness but it's not easy. I knew one teacher who sent the head secretary flowers and the damn things wilted as soon as they sensed her presence. Head secretaries can curdle milk across a wide room and intimidate pit bulls with a scowl so don't have breakfast with them or let them near your dog.

In brief, it's hard to befriend a head secretary. Even other secretaries don't like them. Few people ever win one over and even fewer want to.

As a highly trained guerrilla, you can always go on the attack instead. Steal her supplies from the vault and drive her to distraction. Nothing so infuriates a head secretary as somebody tampering with her supplies. A missing box of paper clips or a ream of copy paper will throw her into a raging tantrum and provide entertainment for the entire office staff.

*Survival Rule:* **Head secretaries are fearsome creatures and should not be crossed in frontal assaults.**

Screw her swivel chair down three inches and she'll think she's shrinking. Download some porno flicks into her computer when she isn't looking and call them up so they'll be on screen when she gets back from her coffee break. You can start rumors that she's having an affair with the principal though more than likely they won't be just rumors.

Every time you pass her desk scoop some papers off into the wastebasket but be careful they aren't payroll records or nobody will get paid on time.

As usual, a disclaimer is required here because not all head secretaries are as described above. Some are civil and pleasant and warm-hearted but I've never actually seen any of this sort myself. If you know of any like this, you might send me their names and I'll record them all on a 3x5 index card for future reference.

In the meantime, play your cards close to your vest when dealing with these people. Don't expose any weaknesses; play dumb. Avoid her if possible; get your mail when she's on her break or, better still, have a friend pick it up and don't ever go into the office at all. Don't comment on her to others as she has an elaborate network of informers and will hear your disparaging words within minutes of your saying them.

Remember, the principal's only a puppet; the head secretary is the puppeteer.

*Why in the world are salaries
higher for administrators
when the basic mission is teaching?*
– Ralph Waldo Emerson

## Chapter Twenty Seven

### PRINCIPALS

Everybody's intimidated by the principal. The kids fear him because he's the final arbiter, the one who holds expulsion hearings and recommends long prison sentences, and the teachers fear him for the same reasons. Nothing produces greater anxiety in teachers and kids alike than the chilling words, "The principal wants to see you."

Well, the truth is the principal is usually just as intimidated by staff and kids as they are by him because he's worried about how his own bosses will perceive him. If he screws up he'll have the superintendent and the whole school board on his neck and he knows it. His mantra is don't make waves and that's why he'll back and fill and kowtow to every pressure group and irate parent that confronts him.

Remember, the principal got to be the principal in the first place by politicking, that is, by bobbing and weaving and obsequiousness and making the right friends and so on. He's not the best teacher but he is an artful dodger.

This means he will automatically lack backbone since people with lots of backbone find it hard to tolerate the half-wits and nincompoops you must befriend if you are to secure their favor. As a result you end up with a gutless guy who puts up a bold front with underlings and bows and scrapes whenever anyone appears on the scene who might cause trouble for him. In other words, you get a politician, a humbug, a lickspittle, a sycophant or something similar.

What you don't get is a fearless, innovative, imaginative leader who is able to run the place with any kind of efficiency.

Some principals are so insecure they never leave their offices. They sneak in early in the morning and don't come out until everybody's gone at night. They rule by memo and the school PA system. They interrupt classes every fifteen minutes with some trivial announcement just to let you know they're still around, but you still don't see them. After a while you begin to think maybe it's another Wizard of Oz trick and the Wiz is doing a number on you.

Another type is the sneaky bozo who prowls around the school spying on everybody. He loves to "write people up." He's forever putting derogatory letters in teachers' files, pops in and out of johns, tiptoes up and peers in classrooms, drops in on the teachers' lounge to see if he can catch somebody zonked out in the Lazy Boy Lounger, patrols the parking lots looking for dopers, and generally makes a nuisance of himself.

*Survival Rule:* **Let the principal know you're onto him. Hint at guerrilla warfare, conspiracies, cabals.**

Even worse are the principals who apply pressure on their teachers to change grades. They do this because principals hate it when too many kids fail, as it looks bad for them. Parents get pissed, board members scowl and demand explanations, lawsuits are filed. People demand accountability and threaten those responsible for an excessive failure rate. In other words, the word to the staff is don't fail any more kids than absolutely necessary no matter what.

So, what do you do with such a person? Do you let him "adjust" your grades? Do you throw away your integrity and kowtow? Of course not. As a proud professional, you resist the old fool and stand up for honor and right.

But you have to hang tough and persevere because it's an ongoing problem in schools all across America, a continuing assault on every teacher's integrity. Every semester without fail certain of our teachers at Mackenzie would be hauled before whichever unprincipled principal happened to be in residence at the moment and rebuked for failing too many kids. Naturally, Big Mack's battle-scarred teachers developed strategies for resisting such insulting interference, as you will see in one incident I personally witnessed involving Marv Nussbaum.

"See here, Nussbaum," principal Snarf said, "you've failed almost 50% of this class. How do you explain that?"

"It's simple. They didn't get passing grades."

"You mean you didn't give them passing grades."

*Survival Rule:* **Insist on grading your own students; it's your chance to nail the rascals.**

"No, I mean they didn't earn passing grades. I don't give grades; people earn them. These kids were absent more than they were there; they averaged less than 50% on fourteen tests, didn't do an assigned report, and averaged one homework assignment out of four. So they flunked."

"You can't flunk half the class, Nussbaum!" Snarf shouted. "If a teacher fails half her kids it means there's something wrong with that teacher."

"Bullshit. It means there's something wrong with the kids."

"Don't say that!" Snarf said, looking around nervously to be sure they weren't overheard. "Every child can learn and it's the teacher's fault when they don't." He tapped a manila folder on his desk. "I don't imagine you'd want that in your file, would you, Nussbaum?"

"I don't care what you do with it," Marv said.

Snarf tried a different tack once he saw intimidation wouldn't work. "You gotta see this from my point of view, Marv," he pleaded. "If we fail too many kids, the brass will get on my neck. It looks bad. Parents get mad, all the nut cakes out there raise Cain. Don't forget, we're accountable now, everybody is. We gotta cover our ass, Marv. You know how it is, right?"

"Sixty-percent is passing in my class. None of these kids got 60% averages."

"But your standards are too high!" Snarf said. "Take the kids where you find them. If they're not too sharp, then you have to lower your standards to accommodate them. Give easier tests. Don't take off for spelling. Lower the passing score. Mark on a curve. Hell, Nussbaum, that's what everybody else does."

*Survival Rule:* **Never lower your standards. If somebody doesn't meet them, flunk him.**

"Maybe so but I'm not everybody else," Marv said. He

rose and moved to the door where he turned back and made this speech. "Look, I don't make a lot of money and I don't have a promising future but I do have a smidgen of integrity. I also have tenure. I know I can refuse to allow anyone to change my grades and you can't fire me. I'm the one who taught that class and I know the kind of work those kids did and nobody can come along and tell me I have to change earned grades for unearned ones. I refuse to do that. Don't call me in again for this crap."

With those parting words, Marv took his leave. Principal Snarf was left with his mouth agape and he snapped it shut and glowered at me.

"Why, he can't talk to me like that! You're a witness, Keliher. You heard what he said. He'll never teach in this town again...!"

I gathered up my stuff and left him fuming and ran into Marv in the hall.

"Nice job, Marv," I said, "but weren't you a little rough on him?"

"He's a fool," he said. "And dangerous. I let him off easy."

And do you know what? I think he did.

If you decide to follow Marv's example and stand tall in this grading business, then you need to know a few things. For one, keep good records and lots of them. Make sure your record book is up to date and accurate because you'll be challenged by some thug's attorney when they haul you before the school board for claiming you have rights they don't think are yours.

Give a lot of tests. You'll want to have solid evidence the kid's a failure and nothing works better than a very long procession of F's in the old grade book. Blank spaces look even better because they indicate the kid didn't even turn anything in.

Run his attendance record alongside his grades so they'll appear together and further cement the idea that he not only deserves his F but should probably do a little time in the bargain. See if you can attach his parole record to the grade book and throw in a urine sample for good measure.

Save his test papers complete with all the wrong or missing answers to counter charges that you made mistakes or deliberately set out to get him with phony grades. Keep proof that you offered make-up work that he refused to do. Show that you secretly taped fourteen chapters together in his textbook and the tape was never broken. Keep daily anecdotal records specifying particular outrages and have them verified by classmates willing to sell out for better grades.

It's a tedious business, all in all, but if you do your homework not even the gods will prevail against you and the clown will flunk and remain an ignorant lout and they'll fire the principal for failing kids beyond his quota and justice will triumph.

If you've got a real jackass for your principal like those described above, you've got a problem. Actually, this is precisely the place for a concerted, all-out attack on administrative malfeasance so round up your guerrilla accomplices and put the guy in his place once and for all.

Sign his name to love notes written to the drama teacher and leave them in conspicuous places. Make up phony phone messages to him from the substance abuse control center advising him of the next meeting and leave them around the office. Send anonymous letters to the school board asking that he be made to explain the peepholes in the girls' locker room wall, and so on. (If there aren't any holes in said walls, drill some. I can't do everything for you, you know.)

See that he knows he's under siege. Sign your handiwork with a bloody handprint. Call yourself the Masked Avenger or The Doomsday Squad and hint at violence. You can have the clown on the defensive in no time and keep him so busy trying to clear his name he won't have time for you.

However, if you aspire to be a principal yourself someday you'll have to forget the foregoing and change those grades or, better still, just hand your record book to the principal and let him have his way with it. You'll feel vaguely unclean afterwards but he'll regard you as one of the boys and a real team player and that's worth something, isn't it?

So of what use is the principal? Do we really need this guy? Yes, actually, we do. His chief job is to keep order in the building and the campus safe. Fire him if the school is overrun with thugs and hall-wanderers, as it's his fault for not running them the hell out. He needs to supervise his staff and make sure they're on time and not letting the kids run amuck. He can also be a greeter, a guy in a suit who glad hands incoming visitors and handles the PR stuff. He can do lunch.

He must not hold long, boring meetings or conduct workshops, seminars, retreats of any kind. He must never mouth the words teacher accountability. Since he doesn't do much real work, it hardly seems fair to pay him the same as a classroom teacher, but we don't want to be unkind, either.

Set his salary at, say, a grand below a maximum teacher, that seems about right.

I might add here that recent attempts to hold principals accountable for the academic success of their schools are absurd, unfair, and dumb. Principals have never had any control over how much learning takes place. If you fire a principal this year for low achievement, you'll have to fire his replacement two years later and so on ad infinitum. We know this is true because the status quo never changes.

The main thing about principals, then, is that they're mostly nondescript people who are very insecure and feel constantly threatened by everybody. The best defense against them is a good offense. If they monkey around with you, launch that guerrilla war we talked about and make them rue the day they dared to cross swords with you, by god.

*The first thing you must do is get their attention; that's what the hickory stick is for.*
– Anon

## Chapter Twenty Eight

### HOW TO DOWNSIZE YOUR SUPERINTENDENT – AND WHY

He's overpaid and under worked. You won't find an original idea in a skyscraper full of these guys yet they routinely draw handsome salaries in excess of a two hundred grand a year and perks that include chauffeured limos, free rent, first-class hotels and air travel, stock options, retirement bonuses, relocation allowances, and more.

In truth, the average superintendent can best serve his district by abolishing his position and remanding his excessive salary to the general fund where it can be used for something worthwhile like new computers for the teachers or a bank of metal detectors.

Superintendents do more harm than good because each feels obligated to do something to justify his pay and secure his position, and that means he looks for something to change, something he can hang his hat on and call his own.

For example, one new superintendent in this mode espied a wall map of the city schools in Detroit once and a Grand Idea was born.

"The schools are all spread out randomly over the city," he said. "There's no symmetry. Why not put them together in clumps and call them, uh..."

"Clumps!" a nearby sycophant shouted.

And so the city was duly divided into eight Clumps with each headed up by a Chief Clump and an elected ten-member board of Associate Clumps who ran the individual units.

A great deal of effort went into this scheme. Public relations people were hired to launch an assault on the public and handle the media and a slew of press announcements heralded the innovation far and wide. Committees were formed and meetings were held hither and yon. Truckloads of jelly donuts were eaten by participants, reams of paper were printed, stapled, and folded, and citizen groups arranged themselves by ethnic background, race, creed, IQ, religion, and weight and each demanded an equal voice in the operation of his own particular Clump.

At last, after two or three years of screwing around, circles were drawn on the city wall map encasing the Clumps and each was given a number. Henceforth, the Clumps were known as Clump One or Clump Eight, etc., and the entire plan was declared a smashing success.

And what was the end result of all this?

Nothing. Less than nothing, in fact, as the schools continued to decline exactly as before. Dropouts dropped out, hooky players multiplied, teacher assaults mounted, chaos spread everywhere. Millions of dollars were spent on salaries for eight new assistant superintendents and their extensive staffs, buildings were built or leased to house everybody, eighty or so additional school board members were turned loose in the community to stir up trouble, and the only changes brought about by this exercise in stupidity were for the worse.

All this happened years ago in Detroit but it appears that no one learned anything from it. At about that same time, New York hatched a similar scheme and decentralized their schools in favor of community control and a lessening of the bureaucracy that stood in the way of real change. We all know the stunning successes that burg has enjoyed in its public schools since, of course.

Los Angeles runs a continuing scheme in the very same foolishness as they've spent the past several years installing a plan dubbed LEARN, an acronym standing for Los Angeles Educational Alliance for Restructuring Now. The chief purpose of this idea is to increase local control and divide the city into semi-autonomous Regions exactly as was done in New York and Detroit decades earlier.

Nobody in Los Angeles knows, of course, that this plan failed utterly in both places and wasted millions of dollars. Or do they know and just don't care? The point is, the whole boondoggle started when the new superintendent wanted to make a name. The schools—and the kids—would have been better off if this humbug had never been hired.

*Survival Rule:* **The superintendent is not your friend, undermine his ass every chance you get.**

More blundering. L.A. had a superintendent named Ruben Zacarias who came out with a list of the 100 worst schools in the city and threatened to fire the principals who were unable to raise achievement scores to new highs. Ironically, Dr. Zacarias had been the principal of one of these schools for three years and left it as he found it, i.e., one of the worst schools in town.

There are endless such stories. L.A. hired a retired admiral and paid the guy $300,000 a year and $71,000 in perks. The sailor knew nothing about education so his first act was to hire an assistant who knew which way was up at wages approaching his own. The new hired hand did all the work and Brewer went into semi-retirement. The school board finally wised up and fired him after two years and he fled with a $500,000 settlement. No test scores have changed, of course.

Such tales are endless. Remember, there are about 15,000 school districts in the country and each one has a superintendent. If these guys are worth anything why are the schools so screwed up? Why don't they fix them? If underperforming teachers and principals should be fired, why not underperforming superintendents?

Low test scores? Fire the superintendent and all of his henchmen. Under achievement? Can the super. Low graduation rates? Throw the bum out. School violence rising? Cashier his ass. If it's good enough for teachers and principals, why not for incompetent and ineffective superintendents?

Still more. We get two myths for one when we examine the Kansas City schools in recent years and see how razor sharp superintendents and cool cash can raise achievement. The system was heavily segregated and in an effort to attract white suburban kids to the city schools the feds pumped in $2 billion to rebuild everything. They soon had brand-new campuses on every corner, new furniture, athletic stadium with Olympic-size pools, unlimited chalk and #2 pencils, French chefs in every lunchroom, and on and on.

There's more. KC wanted to make sure they had crackerjack leadership so they hired nineteen superintendents over some thirty years. They even had two or three supers at the same time on occasion. Surely, all this brainpower and vast experience would raise everybody's achievement, integrate the place, and make the KC schools the showcase of American education. Alas, nothing changed as predicted.

To be fair, conduct a study of your superintendent to see if he's worth keeping on the job. Do a background check and see if he's wanted anywhere, as a lot of these guys are on the lam. Post video cameras in his office and see what he actually does in there all day. Hire an efficiency expert and have him do a time study on the super. Put a tail on him when he goes off to attend vague "meetings" somewhere to see if he's really playing golf. Go over his expense accounts, check the books, bug his phone. Few superintendents in the country could stand such scrutiny—and least of all yours.

And while you're at it, send a hatchet man through the Central Office and have him fire every other person he meets to clear out some of the deadwood downtown. It's reported half of all educators do no teaching, a situation that exists in no other industrialized country anywhere, and it's time we fired these hangers-on and did right by those who actually teach.

In a word, no superintendent anywhere ever has any special effect on those under his direction. No test scores rocket into the skies, hooky players don't play hooky less often, dropouts drop out right on schedule, nothing changes.

Not so? Name the success. Chicago? Detroit? New York? L.A.? Hawking's Law again: if you never see it it's not there.

Your superintendent is more a political animal than an educator, always on the move, never staying too long in one place lest you discover his real self. He's often shifty-eyed and looks over his shoulder a lot and smells of garlic. On the plus side, he's usually a snappy dresser.

So act accordingly. Downplay the superintendent's role. Move him to a smaller office. Cut his personal staff from dozens to a gofer and a part-time secretary. Take away his limo. Install a time clock and make him punch in along with the clerical help. When his contract expires give him a job as a classroom teacher and let him do something productive for a change.

Everybody, and especially the teachers, will be better off when he's gone and can no longer meddle. Without a constant flow of interference and inane make-work projects from the Central Office, the teachers should be able to increase their efficiency levels dramatically.

Don't hire a new superintendent; instead, rotate the job among the teachers by drawing straws. It really won't make a shred of difference.

> *Education:*
> *That which discloses to the wise*
> *and disguises from the foolish*
> *their lack of understanding.*
> – Ambrose Bierce

## Chapter Twenty Nine

### HOW ONE VICTIM GOT EVEN

We continue to disintegrate on all fronts.

A friend told me an interesting story recently when a group of us met after school to assuage our grief at a local pub. It seems the principal of one of our infamous junior high schools was successful in getting a transfer to another school after several years of staving off an entire community of rabid dissidents.

They held the usual tea in the school library and everyone went through the motions of wishing him well. Sundry enemies who had been at his jugular a few days ago made laudatory speeches assuring one and all that they had enjoyed working with him, etc.

He also made a speech. He told them how he'd miss working with them, what an ennobling experience it had been, and how he was looking forward to his new challenge. They gave him a cheap briefcase.

Late that night he donned his camouflaged fatigues, returned to the school, crept up to the window of his erstwhile office—and pissed on the building.

*The vanity of teaching often tempts a man to forget he is a blockhead.*
— Lord Halifax

## Chapter Thirty

### TEACHER TYPES – AN OVERVIEW

Teachers come in all sizes, colors, religions, dispositions, and IQs. It helps to know one from another so you can anticipate them and, to that end, I've compiled some sketches of selected teachers so you'll know what to expect from each. They're classified by subject matter because similar people are drawn to like interests so that English teachers will share the characteristics that made them become English teachers and not phys ed. majors. While these observations are necessarily general, they're not all that far off the mark overall.

### Art Teachers

Easy to spot because they often wear berets and outlandish costumes and display a color sense unknown to their fellows. Most have been to France or are planning a trip there soon. They will be more liberal than conservative, probably more familiar with voodoo magic than most, likely to wear amulets to ward off evil spirits, and unpredictable

They will also be more interesting than some others, more talented and creative and original in thought and deed. Few of them ever get promoted because of these severe liabilities that are considered anathema in administrators and, indeed, are seldom found in their ranks.

Art teachers are fun at parties, too.

## Business Teachers

Who says stereotypes don't work? Business teachers teach bookkeeping, typing, filing, copy machine mechanics, business law, retailing sales and other fascinating subjects that so enthrall teen-age minds. These guys are punctual, orderly, neat, and predictable. Principals often pick them to head up committees because they take good notes. In any group, a business teacher is always assigned secretarial duties because, well, nobody else wants to do it. Besides, would it make any sense to assign the job to the welding teacher with somebody sitting there who takes 200 words a minute in shorthand?

Many business teachers have businesses on the side or elaborate business backgrounds and are handy to have around when tax questions arise or stock market info is needed. Some of them can get things for you wholesale.

They can be fun at parties, too, but usually less so than arty types who have fewer inhibitions.

## Counselors

Good partygoers if properly primed with assorted mysterious substances to steady their nerves but subject to rambling and often irrational conversation if not on something. Avoid sudden moves around them.

## English Teachers

Often smug and hosting superior attitudes because they know how to parse a sentence and just about nobody else does, English teachers take an unseemly glee in finding grammatical errors in others' writings. These guys pore over every publication in search of infelicities, especially in stuff that comes from the principal's office. Since many principals are borderline illiterates, English teachers are provided an endless supply of gaffes for their entertainment and peals of laughter may be heard emanating from the lounge with each new memo.

They also have one of the hardest jobs in the entire school system. There is no more grueling work than correcting writing assignments written by people who can't write a lick. Just reading these papers is nearly impossible since none of them uses punctuation that you'd recognize, sentences start and stop wherever the writer pleases, spelling is ignored completely, penmanship is utterly illegible, and mistakes so abound that you can wear out a brand-new red pen grading a single day's output.

However, theirs is also the most important job in the school. No other subject compares with English in its overall importance and they know it. It's too bad the kids don't.

English teachers are great company but don't let them see any samples of your writing if you can help it.

## Foreign Language Teachers

Almost all have accents and take special delight in talking to each other in unknown languages while everybody worries that they're talking about them. Many are from foreign countries themselves and have interesting customs to share with their colleagues. One French teacher from Haiti was well versed in voodoo and raised a ruckus when he was caught in his darkened room with burning candles, chicken entrails, and a doll wearing the principal's likeness and a lot of hatpins. The superintendent was urged to fire him but he declined to do so on the grounds that he didn't want hatpins sticking in his own ass.

Most foreign language teachers are traditionalists because they know the only way to learn a language is to study like hell. There's no room for gimmicks or fads in learning French or German, no panaceas, no shortcuts. You memorize and practice endlessly and conjugate those verbs or you don't learn the language.

Foreign language teachers are interesting people, as they're often widely traveled and they're entertaining and add to a good party.

## **Math and Science Teachers**

Peas in a pod. Precise, orderly thinkers with a penchant for detail and accuracy, science and math types are all caught up in chalk dust and test tubes. They love theory and mysterious symbols and the smell of burning sulfur. Like English teachers, they take pride in knowing obscure stuff but they get fewer chances to show off their knowledge since nobody but other math and science people ever bring up these subjects.

These guys usually dress worse than art teachers because they use other scientists as role models and few of them know much about fashion. A lab coat is haute couture for these types. They wear sensible shoes and acid holes in their shirts and read a lot of Ray Bradbury stuff. They tend to abstract thinking so don't care about things that might interest you unless you're one of them.

They never go to parties.

## Phys Ed. Teachers

Everybody's favorite whipping boy. Who doesn't make fun of the coaches? Some charge they can't read, some that they can't write, and some that they can't do either. Their spoken English is studded with sports clichés like nice guys finish last or when the going gets tough it's time to bug out. They swear a lot and most favor little cigars that are cheap and smell like it. All wear whistles around their necks and grimy sweatshirts.

They love all sports and admire athletes but most are totally out of shape themselves with sunken chests and bellies o'er hanging strained belts. They're easily winded and lack endurance. They like sports, beer, girls, and cigars pretty much in that order and they're the best party animals of all since they've devoted their lives to that pastime.

Most of them are soon promoted as they make up the chief supply of incipient administrators, a factor that may have something to do with the lamentable state of education nowadays.

## Social Studies Teachers

Liberal and Democrats as a rule, these teachers are likely to be more rabid than some others. They're into politics and causes. They favor such things as pro-choice movements, labor unions, welfare programs, anti-war sentiments, and similar people-oriented ideas because they've had special training in reason and logic and can tell right from wrong. They're smart and tough and opinionated, a combination that bodes well for survival in today's schools.

These teachers are also more likely to make trouble for the administration as they love fomenting revolutions and uprisings and take delight in undermining authority. They're also my kind of people, a fact that should be obvious considering the tone of this book.

Social studies teachers like drinking beer and arguments. They party well.

## Administrators

The administration generally doesn't socialize with underlings because the teachers seldom invite them to parties, after school drinks, trysts, and similar entertainments. Administrators are a musty lot generally and tend to lack a sense of humor, tell unfunny jokes that produce forced laughs and awkward moments, and scowl a lot. They like each other and perks. In any case, they're too stodgy to enjoy a good party; don't invite them.

*Education is not filling a pail
but the lighting of a fire.*
– Wm. Butler Yeats

## A SURVIVAL KIT

Teachers today have to be ready for any eventuality and that means having the tools required to cope with crises of every description. In other words, every teacher should have a professionally designed survival kit similar to the one described below.

### CONTENTS
Blood Type
Briefcase
Collapsible Crutch
Ear Plugs
First Aid Kit
Hunting Knife
Layman's Guide to the Law
Lunch
Pepper Spray
Pointer Sans Rubber Tip
Prozac
Rope
Rubber Gloves
Safety Glasses
Tape Recorder
Tourniquet
Transfer Applications
Voodoo Dolls w/Pins

### OPTIONAL
.25 cal. Automatic
Gas Mask
Kevlar Vest

Most of these items need no explanation since their uses are obvious. The briefcase should be big enough to hold everything. The pepper spray should be maximum strength, the knife serrated and at least a foot long, the rope sturdy. The tape recorder is to tape conversations with administrators and irate parents for use in future lawsuits.

The Prozac should be taken as needed, i.e., often; the pointer carried in hand at all times. The gun, vest, and gas mask are recommended but not required unless you're teaching at Mackenzie High or someplace just like it.

Feel free to improvise. Add a Bible for administering the Last Rites, a large crucifix to ward off evil, a phial of holy water, lucky charms, a wistful sigh. Always keep your survival kit close at hand for it's sure to come in handy one day.

## A FINAL WORD

There have been three major breakthroughs in the field of education in the last half of the 20th century that revealed new truths to the perceptive. One of these is the Coleman Report, another is Project Follow-Through, and the third is my own discovery that school reform is impossible.

We can start with the Coleman Report. Everyone knows of it but very few know what's in it. It is the quintessential answer to the charge that so-called "bad" teachers are the cause of our kids' failures. Others claim the schools are to blame for failing students due to inadequate buildings, insufficient supplies, or ineffective curricula, but the Coleman Report found none of these at fault.

In 1966 James Coleman studied 600,000 children in 4,000 schools and learned that two key factors were found to predict success in our schools: family background and the socioeconomic level of the school.

There. Family background and income, nothing else counts as much as these factors. It's self-evident; look at schools anywhere and you'll see direct evidence of Coleman's conclusions: kids in better schools and neighborhoods do better than kids less fortunate. Teachers, buildings, supplies, curricula play minor roles.

Tell the "bad teachers" crowd to do their homework and read the Coleman Report. They won't, of course, because they're morons. In fact, the Coleman Report should be required reading for every educator, politician, and parent in the land and our efforts should be governed by its findings. If nothing else, we might at least focus the blame for low achievement where it properly belongs, i.e., on the students themselves and their own karma.

To this point I've painted a fairly dreary picture of our public schools but I can leave you with some hope in spite of all that's gone before. There are answers to be found, ways to raise achievement levels that will actually work, but informed teachers, school board members and parents need to do their own homework to make this happen.

I refer to Project Follow-Through, among the largest and least known of studies anywhere—and one of the most important ever undertaken in the field of education. It came out of Head Start in 1967 when educators were concerned that the program's benefits seemed to disappear by the time kids reached the third grade. To learn why it was decided to devise a study to determine the most effective teaching methodology, one that actually raised achievement levels.

Twenty-four of the principal methodologies in use were examined involving nearly thirty years, 170 communities, 700,000 students, and a billion dollars. Of the selected teaching methodologies, twenty-one were found to either produce no effect whatever on achievement scores or succeeded in bringing scores down.

Only three of the methodologies tested raised achievement levels: Direct Instruction, High Schools That Work, and Success For All.

All three are content-oriented, traditional methodologies with a heavy emphasis on drill and teacher–lead instruction. The curriculum is rigid, often actually scripted, and followed line by line by the teacher. Lessons are planned with specific content goals and allow for little variation. In short, these successful methods are not unlike the model used throughout history, a traditional one with nary a mention of self-esteem and wholesome attitudes.

Chief among these methods is Direct Instruction started by Siegfried Engelmann in 1967. It is the same methodology favored 7,000 years ago when teachers taught and students listened. No circled chairs, no group stuff, no busywork but lots of intellectual elbow grease and empty containers of midnight oil. If raising achievement levels is your goal, Direct Instruction is for you.

Look up the Coleman Report, Project Follow-Through and Direct Instruction. A brief summary of each will do you and your charges a world of good.

Finally, as we saw earlier, school reform is not possible. The plain truth is that there is nothing wrong with our public schools. What we see today is the norm; it is what we always see and should expect. From John Dewey's introduction of the so-called progressive movement in 1899 to today's exit exams, we've seen a full century of school reform failures because we can't change the natural order of things. Not a single one has succeeded, nothing has changed, reality looms at last.

Objective-based Instruction and all similarly focused methodologies are ciphers or even counter productive and bear much of the blame for the sorry state of many of our schools and their graduates. Accordingly, Direct Instruction should be adopted nationwide as the methodology of choice because it works.

Vast sums and countless hours of teacher time will be saved, kids won't be used as guinea pigs for the next Whole Language fiasco, and all will benefit from the only methodology ever found that actually does what it advertises.

All school reform movements always fail. Doubters are reminded of the challenge: name a single reform effort that ever succeeded in helping kids learn easier, faster, and better than they currently do.

I'll wait.

The End

www.ingramcontent.com/pod-product-compliance
Lightning Source LLC
Chambersburg PA
CBHW051753040426
42446CB00007B/342